UNITED NATIONS CONFERENCE ON TRADE AND

UNCTAD

2019

HANDBOOK OF
STATISTICS

UNITED NATIONS
Geneva, 2019

The world by development status

- Developing economies
- Transition economies
- Developed economies
- /// Least developed countries (LDCs)

Requests to reproduce excerpts or to photocopy should be addressed to the Copyright Clearance Center at copyright.com.

All other queries on rights and licences, including subsidiary rights, should be addressed to:

United Nations Publications
405 East 42nd Street
New York, NY 10017
United States of America
Email: publications@un.org

Website: shop.un.org

The designations employed and the presentation of material on any map in this work do not imply the expression of any opinion whatsoever on the part of the United Nations concerning the legal status of any country, territory, city or area or of its authorities, or concerning the delimitation of its frontiers or boundaries.

The publication has not been formally edited.

United Nations publication issued by the United Nations Conference on Trade and Development.

TD/STAT. 44

ISBN: 978-92-1-112940-3
eISBN: 978-92-1-003967-3
ISSN: 1992-8408
eISSN: 2225-3270
Sales No.: E.20.II.D.1

Notes

The tables in this handbook represent extractions from or analytical summaries of datasets contained in the UNCTADstat data portal, available at:

http://unctadstat.unctad.org/

UNCTADstat is continuously updated and enhanced, thus providing users with the latest available data. Consequently, the figures from this handbook, which presents statistics at a point in time, may not always correspond with the figures in UNCTADstat.

Basic information on concepts, definitions and calculation methods of the presented data are provided in the boxes titled "Concepts and definitions" in each section and in annex 6.3 of this handbook. Detailed information on the sources and methods used for production of data available in UNCTADstat can be found in the documentation attached to the respective UNCTADstat dataset (UNCTAD, 2019a).

Where the designation "economy" appears, it refers to a country, territory or area. The assignment of economies to specific groups is done for statistical convenience and does not imply any assumption regarding the political or other affiliation of these economies by the United Nations. Likewise, the designations "developing", "transition" and "developed" are intended for statistical convenience and do not necessarily express a judgement about the stage reached by a particular economy in the development process.

Unless otherwise specified, the values of groups of economies represent the sums of the values of the individual economies included in the group. Calculation of these aggregates may take into account data estimated by the UNCTAD secretariat that are not necessarily reported separately. In cases in which an insufficient number of data points are available within a group of economies, no aggregation is undertaken and the symbol (-) is assigned.

Due to rounding, values do not necessarily add up exactly to their corresponding totals.

United States dollars (US$) are expressed in current United States dollars of the year to which they refer, unless otherwise specified. "Ton" means metric ton (1 000 kg).

Due to space constraints, the names of the following countries may appear in abbreviated form: the Plurinational State of Bolivia, the Democratic People's Republic of Korea, the Democratic Republic of the Congo, the Islamic Republic of Iran, Lao People's Democratic Republic, the Federated States of Micronesia, the United Kingdom of Great Britain and Northern Ireland, and the Bolivarian Republic of Venezuela.

The UNCTAD Handbook of Statistics 2019 is available as a printed copy or in PDF format from the UNCTAD website, at http://unctad.org/en/Pages/Publications/Handbook-of-Statistics.aspx.

2019

Handbook
of Statistics

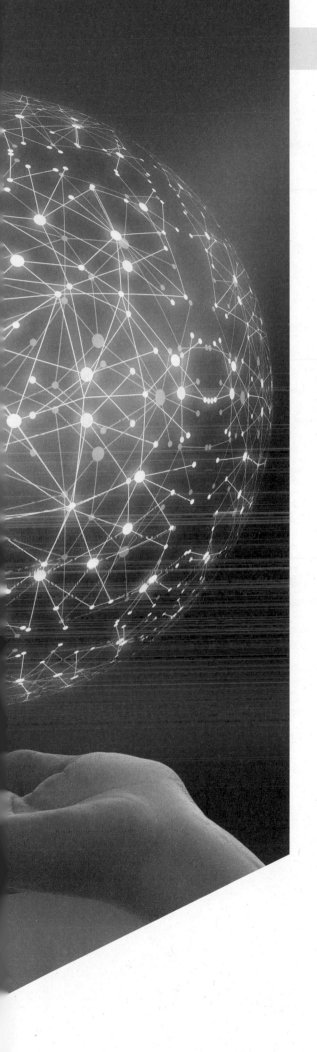

TABLE OF **CONTENT**

List of maps and figures

List of tables

Introduction

The UNCTAD Handbook of Statistics 2019 provides a wide range of statistics and indicators relevant to the analysis of international trade, investment, maritime transport and development. Reliable statistical information is indispensable for formulating sound policies and recommendations that may commit countries for many years as they strive to integrate into the world economy and improve the living standards of their citizens. Whether for research, consultation or technical cooperation, UNCTAD needs reliable and internationally comparable trade, financial and macroeconomic data, covering several decades and for as many countries as possible.

In addition to facilitating the work of the UNCTAD secretariat, the UNCTAD Handbook of Statistics and the UNCTADstat Data Center make internationally comparable sets of data available to policymakers, research specialists, academics, officials from national Governments, representatives of international organizations, journalists, executive managers and members of non-governmental organizations.

This year's edition incorporates several new charts and maps, and also includes for the first time new maritime statistics dealing with port performance: tables showing the number of port calls and the time spent by ships in port, sub-divided into eight market segments (see chapter 5). This update also incorporates the latest population estimates from the United Nations World Population Prospects 2019 (including significant adjustments for Eritrea, Eswatini, Lebanon, Maldives, South-Sudan, Venezuela and Zimbabwe). The urban and rural population estimates are based on the United Nations World Urbanization Prospects 2018.

An online version of the handbook or e-handbook is also available at: http://stats.unctad.org/handbook/. The e-handbook is a fully interactive tool, including maps and charts, that allow readers to directly access the data from the UNCTADstat Data Center associated with each table or chart.

Abbreviations and Symbols

Abbreviations

BPM6	Balance of Payments and International Investment Position Manual, Sixth Edition
BRICS	Brazil, Russia, India, China and South Africa
CIF	cost, insurance and freight
CPI	consumer price index
Dem. Rep.	Democratic Republic
dwt	dead-weight tons
EBOPS 2010	2010 Extended Balance of Payments Services Classification
FDI	foreign direct investment
FMCPI	free market commodity price index
FOB	free on board
GDP	gross domestic product
gt	gross tons
G20	Group of Twenty
HIPCs	heavily indebted poor countries
HS	Harmonized Commodity Description and Coding System
IMF	International Monetary Fund
ITC	International Trade Centre
ISIC	International Standard Industrial Classification of All Economic Activities
LDCs	least developed countries
LLDCs	landlocked developing countries
LNG	liquefied natural gas
LPG	liquefied petroleum gas
LSBCI	liner shipping bilateral connectivity index
LSCI	liner shipping connectivity index
Rep.	Republic
SAR	Special Administrative Region
SIDS	small island developing States
SITC	Standard International Trade Classification
TEU	twenty-foot equivalent unit
UN-OHRLLS	United Nations Office of the High Representative for the Least Developed Countries, Landlocked Developing Countries and the Small Island Developing States
US$	United States dollars
WTO	World Trade Organization

Symbols

0	Zero means that the amount is nil or negligible.
_	The symbol underscore indicates that the item is not applicable.
..	Two dots indicate that the data are not available or are not separately reported.
-	The use of a hyphen on data area means that data is estimated and included in the aggregations but not published.

A dash between years (e.g. 1985–1990) signifies the full period involved, including the initial and final years.

(e)	Estimated data
(p)	Provisional data
(u)	Preliminary estimate

1

International merchandise trade

KEY FIGURES **2018**

Value of
world merchandise
exports
US$19.5 trillion

South-South
share of
global trade
28%

LDCs' share of
global exports
0.98%

NOWCAST **2019**

Growth of world
merchandise trade
-2.4%

1.1 Total merchandise trade

Map 1.1 | **Merchandise exports as a ratio to gross domestic product, 2018**
(Percentage)

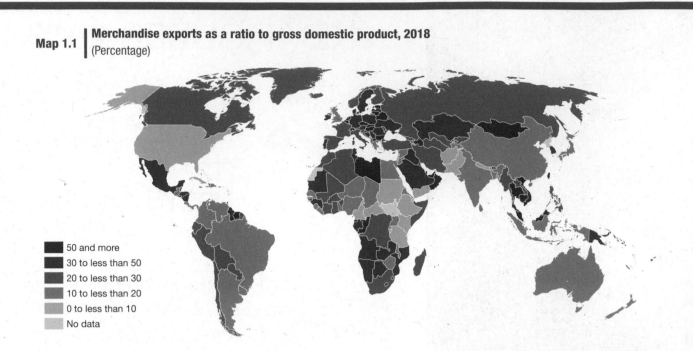

- 50 and more
- 30 to less than 50
- 20 to less than 30
- 10 to less than 20
- 0 to less than 10
- No data

Concepts and definitions

The figures on international merchandise trade in this chapter measure the value of goods which add or subtract from the stock of material resources of an economy by entering or leaving its territory (United Nations, 2011). This definition is slightly different from the definition of trade in goods in the balance-of-payments framework (see section 3.2).

The value of exports is mostly recorded as the free-on-board (FOB) value, whereas the value of imports includes cost (for clearance), insurance and freight (CIF).

The trade balance is calculated as the difference between the values of exports and imports.

Merchandise trade figures from 2014 to 2018, at total product level with partner world, are jointly produced by UNCTAD and the World Trade Organization (WTO).

Global trends and patterns

In 2018, the surge in world merchandise trade recorded the previous year continued. Exports rose by 9.7 per cent and reached a record high of US$19.5 trillion. However, growth is nowcast to halt in 2019 with exports decreasing by 2.4 per cent.

Global exports were distributed in almost equal shares between the 'North' and the 'South'. In 2018, developing and transition economies jointly contributed US$9.3 trillion to the world total, of which US$8.6 trillion came from developing economies. Exports from developed economies added an additional US$10.1 trillion.

In Europe, Central America, Southern Africa and South-Eastern Asian economies, merchandise exports seldom accounted for less than 20 per cent of gross domestic product (GDP), whereas in the Caribbean and in Central and Eastern Africa that rate was typically below 10 per cent.

Figure 1.1.1 | **World merchandise exports**
(Trillions of United States dollars)

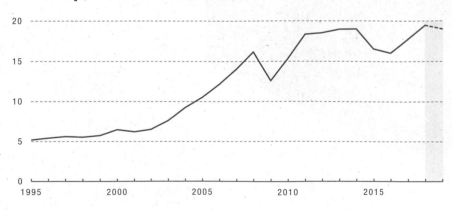

Note: The shaded area indicates UNCTAD nowcasts. For the methodology, see annex 6.3.

Different exposure to the upswing in trade

In 2018, transition economies enjoyed a boost in merchandise exports (22.7 per cent), increasing at almost two and a half times the rate of their imports (9.4 per cent). Africa also experienced high exports growth (14.7 per cent), combined with a slightly slower growth of imports (11.6 per cent). In the other economic groups exports and imports increased in line with the world average, varying between 8 and 11 per cent, with imports growing slightly faster than exports.

Figure 1.1.2 | **Merchandise trade annual growth rates, 2018**
(Percentage)

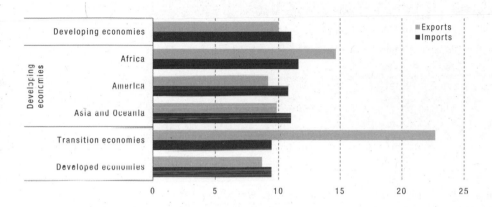

Development of global trade imbalances

For developing and transition economies, the value of the goods exported exceeds the value of goods imported, whereas developed economies are on average net importers. However, over the last five years, the trade surplus in developing countries has diminished from US$455 billion in 2014 to US$335 billion in 2018. By contrast, the surplus of transition economies reached a trough in 2016, at US$72 billion, but has since grown to US$183 billion in 2018. That reversal in trend was mirrored by a shrinkage of the developed economies' deficit until 2016, down to US$634 billion, followed by an increase until 2018 to a level of US$858 billion.

Figure 1.1.3 | **Merchandise trade balance**
(Billions of United States dollars)

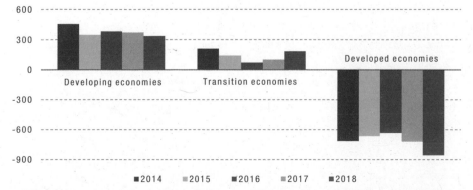

Note: Trade balances do not add up to zero at world level due to CIF included in imports and cross-country differences in compilation methods.

Surge in world trade **continued**

2018:
+9.7%

Transition economies' **exports** grew by
+23%

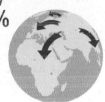

Africa's exports (+15%) growing faster than imports (+12%)

Developed economies' **deficit** continues to **rise**

Table 1.1.1 | Merchandise trade by group of economies

Group of economies	Exports Value (Billions of US$)		Exports Annual growth rate (Percentage)	Imports Value (Billions of US$)		Imports Annual growth rate (Percentage)	Trade balance Value (Billions of US$)	Trade balance Ratio to imports (Percentage)
	2013	2018	2018	2013	2018	2018	2018	2018
World	**18 951**	**19 453**	**9.7**	**18 966**	**19 794**	**10.1**	**-340**	**-1.7**
Developing economies	8 436	8 657	10.0	8 013	8 322	11.0	335	4.0
Developing economies: Africa	591	484	14.7	640	576	11.6	-92	-16.0
Developing economies: America	1 118	1 086	9.2	1 168	1 123	10.8	-37	-3.3
Developing economies: Asia and Oceania	6 727	7 087	9.8	6 205	6 623	11.0	464	7.0
Transition economies	806	674	22.7	616	492	9.4	183	37.1
Developed economies	9 708	10 122	8.7	10 336	10 980	9.4	-858	-7.8
Selected groups								
Developing economies excluding China	6 227	6 170	10.1	6 063	6 186	9.4	-16	-0.3
Developing economies excluding LDCs	8 242	8 466	10.0	7 775	8 051	11.0	415	5.2
LDCs	194	191	11.9	238	271	9.9	-80	-29.4
LLDCs	229	191	17.8	220	215	13.3	-24	-11.1
SIDS (UNCTAD)	28	19	9.5	41	37	6.3	-19	-50.1
HIPCs (IMF)	125	130	10.1	184	178	7.7	-47	-26.7
BRICS	3 384	3 588	11.4	3 134	3 201	14.7	387	12.1
G20	14 191	14 928	9.6	14 521	15 304	10.5	-376	-2.5

Table 1.1.2 | Merchandise trade of least developed countries, main exporters

Economy[a]	Exports Value (Millions of US$)		Exports Annual growth rate (Percentage)	Imports Value (Millions of US$)		Imports Annual growth rate (Percentage)	Trade balance Value (Millions of US$)	Trade balance Ratio to imports (Percentage)
	2013	2018	2018	2013	2018	2018	2018	2018
LDCs	**194 382**	**191 406**	**11.9**	**238 404**	**270 998**	**9.9**	**-79 591**	**-29.4**
LDCs: Africa and Haiti	134 285	110 745	10.8	145 085	134 538	7.7	-23 793	-17.7
Angola	68 247	40 758	17.8	26 331	15 798	9.2	24 960	158.0
Zambia	10 600	9 043	12.9	10 177	9 462	18.5	-419	-4.4
Dem. Rep. of the Congo	6 300	(e) 8 800	(e) 11.4	6 300	(e) 5 200	(e) 6.1	(e) 3 600	(e) 69.2
Mozambique	4 024	(e) 5 196	(e) 10.0	10 099	(e) 6 786	(e) 18.1	(e) -1 590	(e) -23.4
United Republic of Tanzania	4 559	3 982	-3.2	12 091	8 818	-5.2	-4 836	-54.8
LDCs: Asia	59 513	79 957	13.6	91 071	134 342	12.3	-54 385	-40.5
Bangladesh	29 114	39 252	9.5	37 085	60 495	14.5	-21 243	-35.1
Myanmar	11 233	16 640	19.9	12 043	19 347	0.5	-2 706	-14.0
Cambodia	6 666	(e) 13 950	(e) 15.4	9 555	18 780	21.2	(e) -4 830	(e) -25.7
Lao People's Dem. Rep.	2 264	5 295	8.7	3 081	6 164	8.8	-869	-14.1
Yemen	8 300	(e) 2 552	(e) 59.5	13 273	(e) 8 387	(e) 12.4	(e) -5 835	(e) -69.6
LDCs: Islands	583	705	10.4	2 247	2 119	2.1	-1 414	-66.7
Solomon Islands	487	524	4.8	537	(e) 615	(e) 7.6	(e) -91	(e) -14.8
Vanuatu	39	63	35.0	313	350	-5.5	-287	-82.0
Timor-Leste	18	47	99.3	843	565	1.9	-518	-91.7
Comoros	21	42	9.5	284	284	13.0	-242	-85.2
Sao Tome and Principe	13	16	5.7	152	148	0.9	-132	-89.2

[a] Ranked by value of exports in 2018.

Table 1.1.3 | **Leading exporters and importers in developing economies, by group of economies, 2018**

Developing economies: Africa

Exporter (Ranked by value)	Value (Billions of US$)	Share in world total (Percentage)	Annual growth rate (Percentage)
South Africa	94	0.48	5.6
Nigeria	61	0.31	36.2
Algeria	41	0.21	17.0
Angola	41	0.21	17.8
Morocco	29	0.15	13.2
Developing Africa	**484**	**2.49**	**14.7**

Importer (Ranked by value)	Value (Billions of US$)	Share in world total (Percentage)	Annual growth rate (Percentage)
South Africa	(e) 114	(e) 0.57	(e) 12.1
Egypt	72	0.36	16.8
Morocco	51	0.26	14.7
Algeria	46	0.23	0.3
Nigeria	43	0.22	37.5
Developing Africa	**576**	**2.91**	**11.6**

Developing economies: America

Exporter (Ranked by value)	Value (Billions of US$)	Share in world total (Percentage)	Annual growth rate (Percentage)
Mexico	451	2.32	10.1
Brazil	240	1.23	10.2
Chile	75	0.39	9.6
Argentina	62	0.32	5.1
Peru	49	0.25	8.0
Developing America	**1 086**	**5.58**	**9.2**

Importer (Ranked by value)	Value (Billions of US$)	Share in world total (Percentage)	Annual growth rate (Percentage)
Mexico	477	2.41	10.3
Brazil	189	0.95	19.7
Chile	75	0.38	14.9
Argentina	65	0.33	-2.2
Colombia	51	0.26	11.2
Developing America	**1 123**	**5.67**	**10.8**

Developing economies: Asia and Oceania

Exporter (Ranked by value)	Value (Billions of US$)	Share in world total (Percentage)	Annual growth rate (Percentage)
China	2 487	12.78	9.9
Korea, Republic of	605	3.11	5.4
China, Hong Kong SAR	568	2.92	3.4
Singapore	413	2.12	10.6
China, Taiwan Province of	336	1.73	5.9
Developing Asia and Oceania	**7 087**	**36.43**	**9.8**

Importer (Ranked by value)	Value (Billions of US$)	Share in world total (Percentage)	Annual growth rate (Percentage)
China	2 136	10.79	15.8
China, Hong Kong SAR	627	3.17	6.4
Korea, Republic of	535	2.70	11.9
India	514	2.60	14.3
Singapore	371	1.87	13.1
Developing Asia and Oceania	**6 623**	**33.46**	**11.0**

1.2 Trade structure by partner

Map 1.2 | **Main world import flows, 2018**
(Billions of United States dollars)

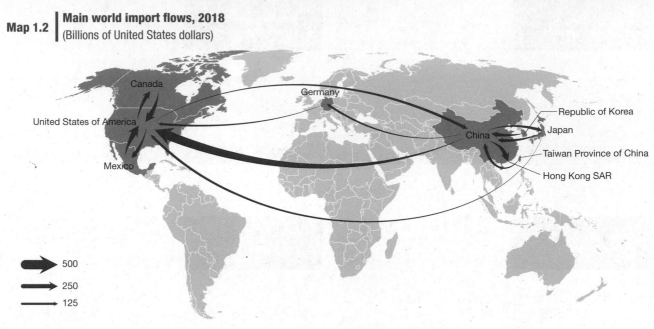

Note: Bilateral imports of US$125 billion or more are shown.

Concepts and definitions

Intra-trade is the trade between economies belonging to the same group. Extra-trade is the trade of economies of the same group with all economies outside the group. It represents the difference between a group's total trade and intra-trade.

In theory, the exports from an economy A to an economy B, should equal the imports of economy B from economy A recorded FOB. In practice, however, the values of both flows are often different. The reasons for these trade asymmetries comprise: different times of recording, different treatment of transit trade, underreporting, measurement errors and mis-pricing or mis-invoicing.

The exports to (imports from) all economies of the world do not always exactly add up to total exports (imports). The difference is caused by ship stores, bunkers and other exports of minor importance.

Main global trade patterns

The world's largest bilateral flows of merchandise trade run between China and the United States of America, and between their respective neighboring economies. In 2018, goods worth US$563 billion were imported by the United States from China. Goods worth US$168 billion also travelled in the opposite direction. China's trade – exports and imports – with Hong Kong Special Administrative Region (SAR), Japan, Taiwan, Province of China, and the Republic of Korea totaled US$1.2 trillion. The United States' trade with Mexico and Canada was worth almost the same amount (US$1.1 trillion).

Intra-regional trade was most pronounced in Europe. In 2018, 69 per cent of all European exports were to trading partners on the same continent. In Asia, this rate was 60 per cent. By contrast, in Oceania, Latin America and the Caribbean, Africa and Northern America, most trade was extra-regional.

Figure 1.2.1 | **Intra- and extra-regional exports, 2018**
(Percentage of total exports)

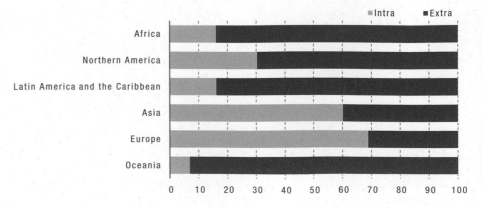

Trade within and between 'hemispheres'

In 2018, goods worth US$6.9 trillion were exchanged between developed economies (North-North trade), whereas merchandise trade among developing and transition economies (South-South trade) amounted to US$5.4 trillion. Exports from developed to developing economies and vice-versa (North-South, and South-North trade) totaled US$6.9 trillion. Thus, for developed economies, trade with developing economies was as important as trade with developed.

Figure 1.2.2 | Global trade flows, 2018

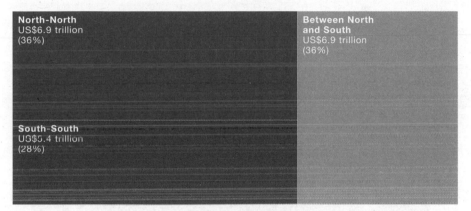

Note: North refers to developed economies, South to developing and transition economies; trade is measured from the export side; deliveries to ship stores and bunkers as well as minor and special-category exports with unspecified destination are not included.

With whom do developing economies mainly trade?

In 2018, developing economies shipped most of their exports to the United States of America (US$1.4 trillion), followed by China (US$1.1 trillion) and other Asian economies. They also sourced most of their imports from the same economies.

Exports from American developing economies were more oriented towards America, especially to the United States of America (US$460 billion), than exports from Africa. For African developing economies, more important export markets were in Asia and Europe, with China (US$54 billion) and India (US$37 billion) as main target economies.

Figure 1.2.3 | Developing economies' main export destinations, 2018
(Billions of United States dollars)

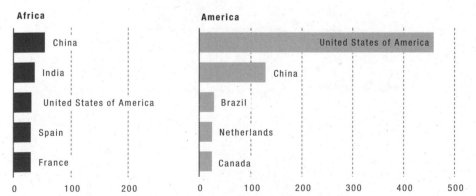

United States of America imported goods exceeding $\frac{1}{2}$ **trillion US$ from China** in 2018

60% of **Asia**'s trade is **intra-regional**

North traded as much **with the South** as with the North:

US$6.9 trillion

Africa's exports **to China:**

US$54 billion in 2018

Table 1.2.1 | Exports by origin and destination, 2018
(Billions of United States dollars)

Origin	Destination						
	World	Developing economies				Transition economies	Developed economies
		Total	Africa	America	Asia and Oceania		
World	**19 414**	**8 064**	**591**	**1 076**	**6 397**	**474**	**10 729**
	(100)	(42)	(3)	(6)	(33)	(2)	(55)
Developing economies	8 649	4 981	342	434	4 205	143	3 480
	(100)	(58)	(4)	(5)	(49)	(2)	(40)
Developing economies: Africa	487	250	77	12	161	3	227
	(100)	(51)	(16)	(2)	(33)	(1)	(46)
Developing economies: America	1 084	415	16	173	226	8	631
	(100)	(38)	(1)	(16)	(21)	(1)	(58)
Developing economies: Asia and Oceania	7 077	4 316	249	249	3 818	133	2 622
	(100)	(61)	(4)	(4)	(54)	(2)	(37)
Transition economies	682	207	23	10	174	112	360
	(100)	(30)	(3)	(1)	(26)	(16)	(53)
Developed economies	10 083	2 876	226	632	2 018	219	6 888
	(100)	(29)	(2)	(6)	(20)	(2)	(68)

Note: Percentage of exports to the whole world in parentheses.

Table 1.2.2 | Exports by origin and destination, selected years
(Billions of United States dollars)

Origin	Year	Destination						
		World	Developing economies				Transition economies	Developed economies
			Total	Africa	America	Asia and Oceania		
World	2008	16 135	5 517	481	866	4 169	564	9 959
	2013	18 997	8 025	640	1 126	6 260	595	10 121
	2018	19 414	8 064	591	1 076	6 397	474	10 729
Developing economies	2008	6 274	3 184	236	373	2 575	123	2 941
	2013	8 454	4 952	359	485	4 109	159	3 285
	2018	8 649	4 981	342	434	4 205	143	3 480
Developing economies: Africa	2008	550	186	55	18	113	3	357
	2013	587	274	86	21	166	3	300
	2018	487	250	77	12	161	3	227
Developing economies: America	2008	910	322	19	199	104	10	569
	2013	1 117	463	20	219	224	10	634
	2018	1 084	415	16	173	226	8	631
Developing economies: Asia and Oceania	2008	4 814	2 675	162	156	2 358	111	2 015
	2013	6 750	4 216	253	244	3 719	146	2 351
	2018	7 077	4 316	249	249	3 818	133	2 622
Transition economies	2008	721	138	12	11	115	144	438
	2013	810	187	14	10	163	137	419
	2018	682	207	23	10	174	112	360
Developed economies	2008	9 140	2 194	233	482	1 479	296	6 579
	2013	9 732	2 886	267	630	1 988	300	6 417
	2018	10 083	2 876	226	632	2 018	219	6 888

Table 1.2.3 | **Top destinations of developing economies' exports**

Destination (Ranked by value of exports)	Rank		2018		
	2018	2013	Value	Share in total exports	Cumulative share
			(Billions of US$)	(Percentage)	(Percentage)
United States of America	1	1	1 416	16.4	16.4
China	2	2	1 142	13.2	29.6
China, Hong Kong SAR	3	3	526	6.1	35.7
Japan	4	4	463	5.4	41.0
India	5	5	350	4.0	45.1
Korea, Republic of	6	6	304	3.5	48.6
Singapore	7	7	222	2.6	51.1
Viet Nam	8	17	215	2.5	53.6
Germany	9	9	212	2.5	56.1
Netherlands	10	10	202	2.3	58.4
China, Taiwan Province of	11	8	166	1.9	60.3
Malaysia	12	11	163	1.9	62.2
Thailand	13	15	158	1.8	64.0
United Kingdom	14	12	155	1.8	65.8
United Arab Emirates	15	13	147	1.7	67.5
Rest of the world	-	-	2 808	32.5	100.0
World	-	-	8 649	100.0	

Table 1.2.4 | **Top origins of developing economies' imports**

Origin (Ranked by value of imports)	Rank		2018		
	2018	2013	Value	Share in total imports	Cumulative share
			(Billions of US$)	(Percentage)	(Percentage)
China	1	1	1 269	15.4	15.4
United States of America	2	2	892	10.8	26.2
Japan	3	3	549	6.7	32.8
Korea, Republic of	4	4	461	5.6	38.4
China, Taiwan Province of	5	6	362	4.4	42.8
Germany	6	5	325	3.9	46.7
Malaysia	7	10	226	2.7	49.5
Singapore	8	9	213	2.6	52.1
Australia	9	11	209	2.5	54.6
India	10	12	194	2.4	56.9
Saudi Arabia	11	7	188	2.3	59.2
Brazil	12	14	186	2.3	61.5
Thailand	13	15	178	2.2	63.6
United Arab Emirates	14	13	162	2.0	65.6
Russian Federation	15	19	160	1.9	67.5
Rest of the world	-	-	2 679	32.5	100.0
World	-	-	8 253	100.0	

1.3 Trade structure by product

Map 1.3 | **Main export products, 2018**

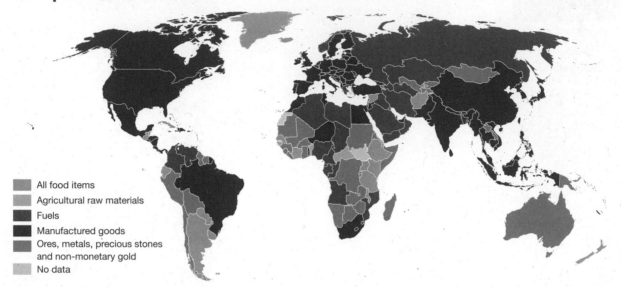

- All food items
- Agricultural raw materials
- Fuels
- Manufactured goods
- Ores, metals, precious stones and non-monetary gold
- No data

Concepts and definitions

The breakdown of merchandise trade by product group is based on the entries in the customs declarations that are coded in accordance with a globally harmonized classification system, called the Harmonized Commodity Description and Coding System (HS). The values of the individual customs declarations have been summed up to the level of product group, error-checked and submitted to the United Nations Statistics Division for integration in the UN Comtrade database (United Nations, 2019a).

The UN Comtrade database contains product breakdowns based on the Standard International Trade Classification (SITC). These have been obtained by conversion of the raw data coded in HS and constitute the main source of the figures presented in this section. For correspondence between SITC codes and the five broad product groups presented in this section, see annex 6.2.

Regional specialization patterns

The global supply of goods to the world market has a marked regional structure. Economies in Northern and Central America; Europe; and Southern, Eastern and South-Eastern Asia export mainly manufactured goods. Economies in other regions are mostly specialized in primary commodities, with the notable exceptions of Brazil, South Africa, Niger and several Northern African economies. The main fuel exporters were located along the northern coast of South America, in Middle and Northern Africa, and Western and Central Asia.

In Africa, primary commodities accounted for three quarters of merchandise exports, in developing America for one half and in developing Asia and Oceania for only one quarter. African exports were dominated by fuels (43 per cent); exports from American developing economies had a relatively high proportion of food (21 per cent).

Figure 1.3.1 | **Export structure of developing economies by product group, 2018**
(Percentage)

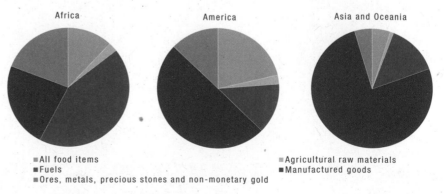

Africa   America   Asia and Oceania

- All food items
- Fuels
- Ores, metals, precious stones and non-monetary gold
- Agricultural raw materials
- Manufactured goods

Note: Non-allocated products are not considered.

Upswing in trade across a whole range of products

The continuing surge of world merchandise trade in 2018 (see section 1.1) was strongly driven by fuels, the exports of which expanded by 22 per cent. Exports of manufactured goods and agricultural raw materials grew by 9 and 8 per cent, respectively, whereas exports of ores, metals, precious stones and non-monetary gold were relatively sluggish, rising by 2 per cent. Food exports increased by 4 per cent.

Figure 1.3.2 | **Annual growth rate of exports by product group, 2018**
(Percentage)

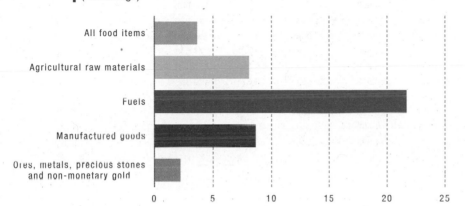

Manufacturing exporters are mostly in

Northern America   Europe   South and east of Asia

What do developing regions trade with others?

Developing regions show considerable differences in their respective trade with the rest of the world. In 2018, exports of goods in developing economies of Asia and Oceania were 7 per cent higher than the value of imports. This trade surplus was driven by manufactured exports and was partially offset by a deficit in other commodity groups. In Africa, the trade structure was entirely different, with manufacturing imports three times higher than exports. Although counterbalanced by surpluses in ores, metals, precious stones and non-monetary gold and in fuels, there remained an overall deficit of 12 per cent. Developing America had a smaller trade deficit than Africa and showed comparatively high net-exports of food.

$\frac{3}{4}$ of Africa's merchandise **exports** were **primary commodities** in 2018

Fuel exports **up** by **22%** in 2018

Figure 1.3.3 | **Developing economies' extra-trade structure, 2018**
(Percentage of exports)

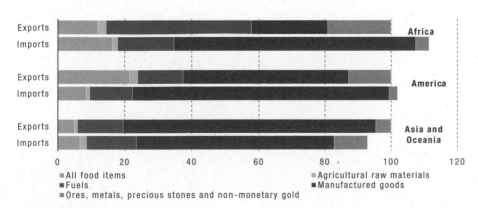

Note: Non-allocated products are not considered.

Africa's manufacturing **imports 3 times** as high as **manufacturing** exports in 2018

Table 1.3 | **Exports by product group, origin and destination, 2018**
(Millions of United States dollars)

All food items

Origin	Destination						
	World	Developing economies				Transition economies	Developed economies
		Total	Africa	America	Asia and Oceania		
World	**1 565 375**	**625 796**	**80 868**	**86 529**	**458 400**	**52 459**	**884 471**
	(100)	(40)	(5)	(6)	(29)	(3)	(57)
Developing economies	629 629	378 586	46 874	39 712	292 000	16 538	233 558
	(100)	(60)	(7)	(6)	(46)	(3)	(37)
Developing economies: Africa	57 714	30 449	14 797	556	15 096	1 491	25 744
	(100)	(53)	(26)	(1)	(26)	(3)	(45)
Developing economies: America	227 554	121 594	10 524	33 522	77 548	5 316	100 071
	(100)	(53)	(5)	(15)	(34)	(2)	(44)
Developing economies: Asia and Oceania	344 361	226 543	21 553	5 634	199 356	9 731	107 744
	(100)	(66)	(6)	(2)	(58)	(3)	(31)
Transition economies	61 371	28 328	7 109	518	20 702	18 476	14 330
	(100)	(46)	(12)	(1)	(34)	(30)	(23)
Developed economies	874 375	218 882	26 886	46 299	145 698	17 445	636 583
	(100)	(25)	(3)	(5)	(17)	(2)	(73)

Note: Percentage of exports to the whole world in parentheses.

Agricultural raw materials

Origin	Destination						
	World	Developing economies				Transition economies	Developed economies
		Total	Africa	America	Asia and Oceania		
World	**276 498**	**138 999**	**8 004**	**10 372**	**120 623**	**4 955**	**131 392**
	(100)	(50)	(3)	(4)	(44)	(2)	(48)
Developing economies	103 922	68 596	3 346	3 716	61 534	1 008	33 689
	(100)	(66)	(3)	(4)	(59)	(1)	(32)
Developing economies: Africa	12 111	8 077	1 117	128	6 833	98	3 931
	(100)	(67)	(9)	(1)	(56)	(1)	(32)
Developing economies: America	26 049	13 917	158	1 988	11 770	281	11 270
	(100)	(53)	(1)	(8)	(45)	(1)	(43)
Developing economies: Asia and Oceania	65 762	46 602	2 071	1 600	42 931	629	18 487
	(100)	(71)	(3)	(2)	(65)	(1)	(28)
Transition economies	14 388	8 068	286	157	7 625	1 521	4 785
	(100)	(56)	(2)	(1)	(53)	(11)	(33)
Developed economies	158 188	62 336	4 373	6 498	51 465	2 426	92 918
	(100)	(39)	(3)	(4)	(33)	(2)	(59)

Note: Percentage of exports to the whole world in parentheses.

Fuels

Origin	Destination						
			Developing economies			Transition economies	Developed economies
	World	Total	Africa	America	Asia and Oceania		
World	**2 438 638**	**1 188 175**	**90 282**	**137 586**	**960 307**	**35 066**	**1 155 481**
	(100)	(49)	(4)	(6)	(39)	(1)	(47)
Developing economies	1 317 945	846 867	52 764	44 954	749 150	2 153	439 557
	(100)	(64)	(4)	(3)	(57)	(0)	(33)
Developing economies: Africa	210 831	104 049	18 726	6 537	78 785	105	105 213
	(100)	(49)	(9)	(3)	(37)	(0)	(50)
Developing economies: America	143 548	74 564	681	30 641	43 242	92	43 842
	(100)	(52)	(0)	(21)	(30)	(0)	(31)
Developing economies: Asia and Oceania	963 566	668 255	33 357	7 775	627 123	1 956	290 502
	(100)	(69)	(3)	(1)	(65)	(0)	(30)
Transition economies	318 162	96 484	3 444	2 473	90 568	24 321	197 258
	(100)	(30)	(1)	(1)	(28)	(8)	(62)
Developed economies	802 531	244 824	34 075	90 159	120 590	8 591	518 666
	(100)	(31)	(4)	(11)	(15)	(1)	(65)

Note: Percentage of exports to the whole world in parentheses.

Manufactured goods

Origin	Destination						
			Developing economies			Transition economies	Developed economies
	World	Total	Africa	America	Asia and Oceania		
World	**13 320 021**	**5 237 044**	**371 784**	**774 765**	**4 090 495**	**354 343**	**7 699 417**
	(100)	(39)	(3)	(6)	(31)	(3)	(58)
Developing economies	5 978 584	3 285 242	219 151	324 688	2 741 404	120 329	2 569 395
	(100)	(55)	(4)	(5)	(46)	(2)	(43)
Developing economies: Africa	112 150	54 003	33 439	3 755	16 809	471	57 564
	(100)	(48)	(30)	(3)	(15)	(0)	(51)
Developing economies: America	529 340	120 228	2 700	94 908	22 620	1 252	407 050
	(100)	(23)	(1)	(18)	(4)	(0)	(77)
Developing economies: Asia and Oceania	5 337 094	3 111 012	183 012	226 026	2 701 975	118 008	2 104 781
	(100)	(58)	(3)	(4)	(51)	(2)	(39)
Transition economies	167 050	41 443	6 136	6 265	29 042	54 696	70 629
	(100)	(25)	(4)	(4)	(17)	(33)	(42)
Developed economies	7 174 387	1 910 358	146 497	443 813	1 320 049	179 319	5 059 393
	(100)	(27)	(2)	(6)	(18)	(3)	(71)

Note: Percentage of exports to the whole world in parentheses.

Ores, metals, precious stones and non-monetary gold

Origin	Destination						
			Developing economies			Transition economies	Developed economies
	World	Total	Africa	America	Asia and Oceania		
World	**1 206 418**	**652 441**	**23 809**	**24 990**	**603 642**	**14 655**	**532 837**
	(100)	(54)	(2)	(2)	(50)	(1)	(44)
Developing economies	557 799	367 943	15 797	11 277	340 870	2 702	181 245
	(100)	(66)	(3)	(2)	(61)	(0)	(32)
Developing economies: Africa	93 252	53 592	9 188	713	43 690	459	33 795
	(100)	(57)	(10)	(1)	(47)	(0)	(36)
Developing economies: America	136 284	77 387	1 083	7 133	69 172	650	58 036
	(100)	(57)	(1)	(5)	(51)	(0)	(43)
Developing economies: Asia and Oceania	328 263	236 965	5 526	3 431	228 008	1 593	89 414
	(100)	(72)	(2)	(1)	(69)	(0)	(27)
Transition economies	54 967	16 047	652	260	15 135	7 190	31 730
	(100)	(29)	(1)	(0)	(28)	(13)	(58)
Developed economies	593 652	268 451	7 360	13 453	247 637	4 763	319 862
	(100)	(45)	(1)	(2)	(42)	(1)	(54)

Note: Percentage of exports to the whole world in parentheses.

1.4 Trade indicators

Map 1.4 | **Trade openness index, 2018**
| (Percentage)

- 50 and more
- 35 to less than 50
- 25 to less than 35
- 15 to less than 25
- 0 to less than 15
- No data

Note: This index measures the importance of international trade in goods relative to the domestic economic output of an economy. Exports are given equal weight to imports.

Concepts and definitions

This section presents different indices that can be used to analyze trade flows and trade patterns over time from the perspective of, for example, relative competitiveness, structure of global exports and imports markets, or the importance of trade for the economy, both for individual economies and for groups of economies.

For information on how the indices in this section are calculated, see annex 6.3. The presented indices are a subset of the trade indices available at UNCTADstat (UNCTAD 2019a).

How important is trade for economies?

In 2018, the economies most open to international trade, as measured by the ratio of the mean of exports and imports to GDP, were relatively small economies in South-Eastern Asia and Eastern Europe, including Hong Kong SAR, Singapore, Viet Nam, Slovakia, Hungary and Slovenia. By contrast, many developing economies in South America and the tropical zones of Africa, as well as some large developed economies, namely the United States of America and Japan, recorded ratios below 15 per cent (i.e., relatively less open).

How did the prices of exports and imports develop?

The terms of trade for both developing and developed economies have remained relatively stable over the last years. In transition economies, they registered an increase of 25 per cent between 2016 and 2018.

Figure 1.4.1 | **Terms of trade index**
| (2015=100)

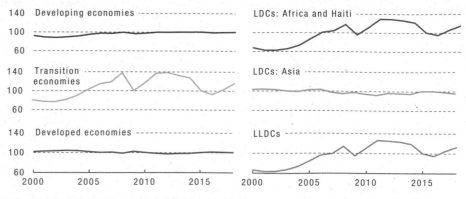

Note: This index indicates by how much the relative price between exports and imports has changed in relation to the base year.

How concentrated is global product supply?

Product groups differ to the degree that global supply is concentrated among exporting economies. The most unequally distributed in 2018 were manufactured exports, as indicated by a market concentration index of 0.19, despite a declining trend since 2015. Exports of primary commodities were more widely spread across suppliers. Index values ranged between 0.12 and 0.14 in 2018 (i.e., relatively less concentrated). For food and agricultural raw materials, concentration of exports has markedly declined over the last 20 years.

Figure 1.4.2 | **Market concentration index of exports**

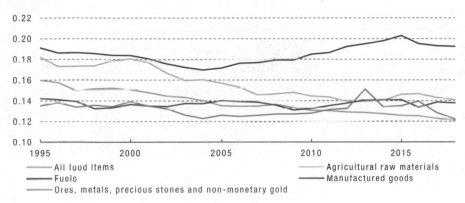

Note: This index measures the extent to which a high proportion of exports are delivered by a small number of economies. It has a value of 1 if all exports originate from a single economy.

How did the trade volume change?

The 0.7 per cent growth of world merchandise trade value in 2018 (see section 1.1) was grounded on a 2.3 per cent increase of export volumes. Export volumes have continuously risen since the 2009 financial crisis. During that period, developing economies saw the strongest increase, leading to an export volume 50 per cent higher than 2009. Developed economies recorded an increase of only 35 per cent. Developing economies' imports rose at a higher pace than their exports (+60 per cent) between 2009 and 2018; for developed economies the pace was slower (+32 per cent).

Figure 1.4.3 | **Volume index of exports and imports**
(2015=100)

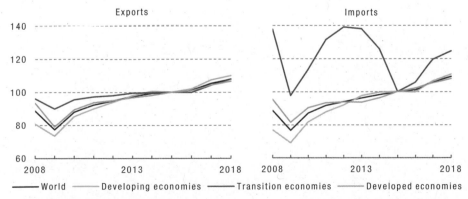

Note: This index indicates the change in exports or imports, adjusted for the movement of prices, relative to the base year.

Hong Kong SAR and **Singapore** are the **most open** economies

Transition economies' **terms of trade** increased by **25%** since 2016

Global **supply** of **manufacturing** has become **less concentrated**

Volume of world merchandise **exports** grew by **2.3%** in 2018

Table 1.4.1 | **Selected trade indices by group of economies**
(2015=100)

Developing economies

Year	Volume[a]		Purchasing power of exports[b]	Terms of trade[c]
	Imports	Exports		
2008	77	81	80	99
2013	98	98	98	100
2017	106	107	107	99
2018	110	110	110	100

[a] See note, figure 1.4.3 above.
[b] This index indicates the change in exports, valued in prices of imports, relative to the base year.
[c] See note, figure 1.4.1 above.

Developing economies: Africa

Year	Volume[a]		Purchasing power of exports[b]	Terms of trade[c]
	Imports	Exports		
2008	77	118	128	108
2013	98	109	129	119
2017	94	104	110	105
2018	98	104	118	113

Developing economies: America

Year	Volume[a]		Purchasing power of exports[b]	Terms of trade[c]
	Imports	Exports		
2008	89	87	98	112
2013	105	94	113	120
2017	99	105	109	103
2018	105	107	113	106

[a] See note, figure 1.4.3 above.
[b] This index indicates the change in exports, valued in prices of imports, relative to the base year.
[c] See note, figure 1.4.1 above.

Developing economies: Asia and Oceania

Year	Volume[a]		Purchasing power of exports[b]	Terms of trade[c]
	Imports	Exports		
2008	74	76	74	97
2013	96	98	94	96
2017	109	108	106	98
2018	113	111	108	98

Transition economies

Year	Volume[a]		Purchasing power of exports[b]	Terms of trade[c]
	Imports	Exports		
2008	138	96	132	137
2013	138	99	132	132
2017	120	104	107	103
2018	124	108	125	116

[a] See note, figure 1.4.3 above.
[b] This index indicates the change in exports, valued in prices of imports, relative to the base year.
[c] See note, figure 1.4.1 above.

Developed economies

Year	Volume[a]		Purchasing power of exports[b]	Terms of trade[c]
	Imports	Exports		
2008	95	93	92	99
2013	94	97	95	98
2017	105	104	105	101
2018	108	107	107	100

Table 1.4.2 | **Selected trade indices, landlocked developing countries**
(2015=100)

Economy	Volume[a]				Purchasing power of exports[b]		Terms of trade[c]	
	Imports		Exports					
	2013	2018	2013	2018	2013	2018	2013	2018
Afghanistan	97	91	85	136	79	145	93	107
Armenia	119	146	87	141	86	155	99	110
Azerbaijan	102	119	103	90	174	113	170	126
Bhutan	74	90	83	94	86	100	104	106
Bolivia (Plurinational State of)	102	93	101	92	143	93	141	101
Botswana	104	84	122	108	113	101	92	93
Burkina Faso	118	134	90	130	90	139	100	107
Burundi	82	88	73	140	67	142	92	101
Central African Republic	55	119	125	170	121	170	96	100
Chad	74	56	90	69	157	87	173	126
Eswatini	104	124	92	94	91	94	99	101
Ethiopia	63	86	91	93	89	87	97	94
Kazakhstan	145	101	110	102	167	126	152	124
Kyrgyzstan	128	119	124	109	122	117	99	107
Lao People's Dem. Rep.	48	101	53	130	54	135	103	104
Lesotho	95	100	89	125	80	113	90	91
Malawi	107	115	112	95	97	92	87	97
Mali	87	116	70	113	75	117	107	104
Mongolia	142	144	65	109	78	140	110	128
Nepal	84	175	119	111	104	100	87	90
Niger	93	100	118	113	133	112	112	99
North Macedonia	88	132	88	148	81	143	92	97
Paraguay	99	119	107	102	94	99	88	97
Republic of Moldova	105	134	96	129	94	128	98	99
Rwanda	87	102	93	141	93	159	100	112
Tajikistan	104	84	112	103	112	119	100	115
Turkmenistan	133	35	117	87	156	97	133	112
Uganda	91	115	101	136	92	129	91	95
Uzbekistan	103	144	106	110	114	113	107	103
Zambia	110	108	127	121	138	124	109	103
Zimbabwe	92	97	111	127	103	127	93	100

[a] See note, figure 1.4.3 above.
[b] See footnote "b", table 1.4.1 above.
[c] See note, figure 1.4.1 above.

2

International trade in services

KEY FIGURES **2018**

Value of world
services exports

US$**5.8 trillion**

Developing
economies' share in
services exports

30%

Share of travel in
services exports

25%

NOWCAST **2019**

Growth of global
trade in services

+2.7%

2.1 Total trade in services

Map 2.1 | **Exports of services as a ratio to gross domestic product, 2018**
(Percentage)

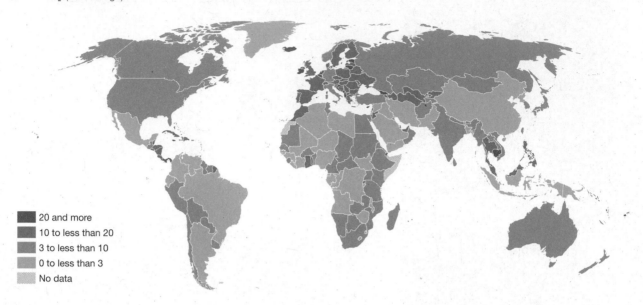

- 20 and more
- 10 to less than 20
- 3 to less than 10
- 0 to less than 3
- No data

Concepts and definitions

In this chapter, in accordance with the concepts of the balance of payments (International Monetary Fund, 2009) and of the national accounts (United Nations et al., 2009), services are understood as the result of a production activity that changes the conditions of the consuming units, or facilitates the exchange of products or financial assets.

International trade in services takes place when a service is supplied in any of the following modes: from one economy to another (services cross the border); within an economy to a service consumer of another economy (consumer crosses the border); or through the presence of natural persons of one economy in another economy (supplier crosses the border) (United Nations et al., 2012).

Trade-in-services figures up to 2018 are jointly compiled by UNCTAD, WTO and the International Trade Centre (ITC).

Growth in world services trade slowing down

After a strong increase of 7.9 per cent in 2017 and 7.7 per cent in 2018, slower growth of 2.7 per cent is nowcast for global services trade in 2019. In 2018, global services trade was valued at US$5.8 trillion, one quarter of the value of total exports and 7 per cent of world GDP. In 2019, it is nowcast to reach US$6.0 trillion.

In 2018, in many economies of Europe, Central America, the Caribbean and South-Eastern Asia, internationally sold services accounted for more than 10 per cent of GDP. Some smaller European economies, such as Luxembourg, Malta or Ireland, and several island economies, such as Aruba, Antigua and Barbuda or the Seychelles, relied to a particularly great extent on services exports. By contrast, in large parts of South America, Western and Central Africa as well as Western and Eastern Asia, services exports amounted to less than 3 per cent of GDP.

Figure 2.1.1 | **World services exports**
(Trillions of United States dollars)

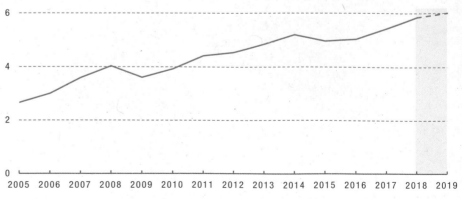

Note: The shaded area indicates UNCTAD nowcasts. For the methodology, see annex 6.3.

American developing economies exhibit slower growth

Looking at the trends by development status and region, transition economies and developing economies in Asia and Oceania recorded strong growth in services exports; more than 10 per cent, exceeding their growth in imports. Africa saw a strong increase in imports (11.9 per cent) combined with slower growth of exports. In the developing economies of America, exports and imports increased at much lower rates, by less than 2 per cent. Exports and imports of developed economies rose at about equal pace as the world total.

International trade in **services accounts** for **7%** of world GDP

Figure 2.1.2 | Services trade annual growth rates, 2018 (Percentage)

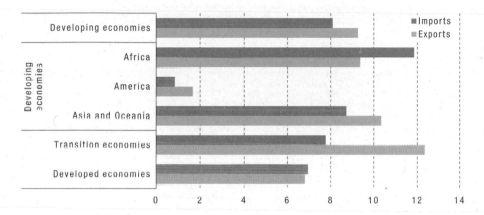

Africa's services imports grew faster than exports: **11.9%**

Leading services exporters

The world's top services exporter in 2018 was the United States of America, with US$828 billion worth of services sold internationally, representing 14 per cent of global services exports. They were followed, at some distance, by three European countries that jointly captured 17 per cent of the world market. China, the leading exporter among developing economies, ranked fifth.

The top five exporting developing economies were Asian, comprising China, India, Singapore, Hong Kong SAR and the Republic of Korea. They held a world market share of almost 15 per cent, the same as all other developing economies combined.

Sluggish services trade in **American developing** economies

Exports: +1.7%

Figure 2.1.3 | Top 5 services exporters, 2018 (Billions of United States dollars)

Exports from developing economies

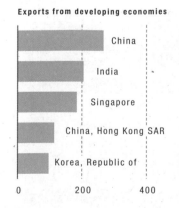

Exports from developed economies

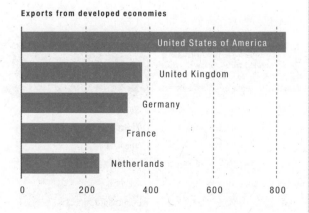

Five Asian developing economies hold **15%** of the world market

Table 2.1.1 | Trade in services by group of economies

Group of economies	Exports Value (Billions of US$) 2013	Exports Value (Billions of US$) 2018	Exports Share in world (Percentage) 2018	Exports Annual growth rate (Percentage) 2018	Imports Value (Billions of US$) 2013	Imports Value (Billions of US$) 2018	Imports Share in world (Percentage) 2018	Imports Annual growth rate (Percentage) 2018
World	**4 841**	**5 845**	**100.0**	**7.7**	**4 726**	**5 604**	**100.0**	**7.4**
Developing economies	1 394	1 738	29.7	9.3	1 745	2 118	37.8	8.1
Developing economies: Africa	99	118	2.0	9.4	177	178	3.2	11.9
Developing economies: America	170	190	3.3	1.7	236	222	4.0	0.9
Developing economies: Asia and Oceania	1 125	1 430	24.5	10.4	1 333	1 718	30.7	8.7
Transition economies	137	137	2.3	12.4	194	158	2.8	7.8
Developed economies	3 310	3 970	67.9	6.8	2 787	3 327	59.4	7.0
Selected groups								
Developing economies excluding China	1 187	1 471	25.2	8.0	1 415	1 593	28.4	6.8
Developing economies excluding LDCs	1 358	1 692	29.0	9.0	1 666	2 041	36.4	8.1
LDCs	36	46	0.8	18.5	79	77	1.4	8.6
LLDCs	39	48	0.8	14.8	65	68	1.2	13.2
SIDS (UNCTAD)	19	25	0.4	9.8	14	16	0.3	2.9
HIPCs (IMF)	29	38	0.7	11.0	55	64	1.1	13.9
BRICS	481	587	10.0	12.6	688	881	15.7	10.7
G20	3 787	4 543	77.7	7.7	3 564	4 311	76.9	7.7

Table 2.1.2 | Leading services exporters and importers by group of economies, 2018

Developing economies: Africa

Exporter (Ranked by value)	Value (Billions of US$)	Share in world total (Percentage)	Annual growth rate (Percentage)	Importer (Ranked by value)	Value (Billions of US$)	Share in world total (Percentage)	Annual growth rate (Percentage)
Egypt	(e) 24	(e) 0.40	(e) 20.6	Nigeria	(e) 31	(e) 0.55	(e) 69.1
Morocco	19	0.32	7.0	Egypt	(e) 19	(e) 0.33	(e) 4.9
South Africa	16	0.27	1.3	South Africa	16	0.29	2.0
Ghana	(e) 8	(e) 0.13	(e) 14.7	Algeria	(e) 11	(e) 0.19	(e) -3.6
Kenya	(e) 5	(e) 0.09	(e) 14.4	Morocco	11	0.19	7.5
Developing Africa	**118**	**2.02**	**9.4**	**Developing Africa**	**178**	**3.18**	**11.9**

Developing economies: America

Exporter (Ranked by value)	Value (Billions of US$)	Share in world total (Percentage)	Annual growth rate (Percentage)	Importer (Ranked by value)	Value (Billions of US$)	Share in world total (Percentage)	Annual growth rate (Percentage)
Brazil	34	0.58	-1.3	Brazil	68	1.21	-0.5
Mexico	(e) 29	(e) 0.49	(e) 5.1	Mexico	(e) 37	(e) 0.66	(e) 0.7
Argentina	14	0.24	-4.2	Argentina	24	0.43	-4.3
Panama	14	0.24	2.7	Chile	(e) 14	(e) 0.25	(e) 5.3
Cuba	(e) 11	(e) 0.18	(e) -5.6	Colombia	(e) 13	(e) 0.24	(e) 7.1
Developing America	**190**	**3.26**	**1.7**	**Developing America**	**222**	**3.96**	**0.9**

Developing economies: Asia and Oceania

Exporter (Ranked by value)	Value (Billions of US$)	Share in world total (Percentage)	Annual growth rate (Percentage)
China	267	4.57	17.0
India	(e) 205	(e) 3.51	(e) 10.7
Singapore	184	3.15	6.6
China, Hong Kong SAR	(e) 114	(e) 1.95	(e) 9.3
Korea, Republic of	(e) 97	(e) 1.65	(e) 10.4
Developing Asia and Oceania	**1 430**	**24.46**	**10.4**

Importer (Ranked by value)	Value (Billions of US$)	Share in world total (Percentage)	Annual growth rate (Percentage)
China	525	9.37	12.3
Singapore	187	3.34	3.0
India	(e) 177	(e) 3.15	(e) 14.2
Korea, Republic of	(e) 124	(e) 2.22	(e) 1.9
Saudi Arabia	86	1.54	10.0
Developing Asia and Oceania	**1 718**	**30.66**	**8.7**

Transition economies

Exporter (Ranked by value)	Value (Billions of US$)	Share in world total (Percentage)	Annual growth rate (Percentage)
Russian Federation	(e) 65	(e) 1.11	(e) 12.3
Ukraine	16	0.27	11.3
Belarus	9	0.15	11.2
Serbia	9	0.15	16.4
Kazakhstan	7	0.12	11.8
Transition economies	**137**	**2.35**	**12.4**

Importer (Ranked by value)	Value (Billions of US$)	Share in world total (Percentage)	Annual growth rate (Percentage)
Russian Federation	(e) 95	(e) 1.69	(e) 6.6
Ukraine	14	0.26	9.3
Kazakhstan	12	0.21	17.7
Azerbaijan	7	0.12	-16.3
Serbia	7	0.12	19.6
Transition economies	**158**	**2.82**	**7.8**

Developed economies

Exporter (Ranked by value)	Value (Billions of US$)	Share in world total (Percentage)	Annual growth rate (Percentage)
United States of America	(e) 828	(e) 14.17	(e) 3.9
United Kingdom	(e) 376	(e) 6.44	(e) 5.5
Germany	(e) 331	(e) 5.67	(e) 7.7
France	(e) 291	(e) 4.99	(e) 5.9
Netherlands	(e) 242	(e) 4.15	(e) 11.4
Developed economies	**3 970**	**67.92**	**6.8**

Importer (Ranked by value)	Value (Billions of US$)	Share in world total (Percentage)	Annual growth rate (Percentage)
United States of America	(e) 559	(e) 9.98	(e) 3.1
Germany	(e) 351	(e) 6.27	(e) 6.2
France	(e) 257	(e) 4.58	(e) 4.7
United Kingdom	(e) 235	(e) 4.20	(e) 10.5
Netherlands	(e) 229	(e) 4.08	(e) 10.9
Developed economies	**3 327**	**59.38**	**7.0**

2.2 Trade in services by category

Map 2.2 | **Changes in services exports by category, 2013–2018**
(Average annual growth rate, percentage)

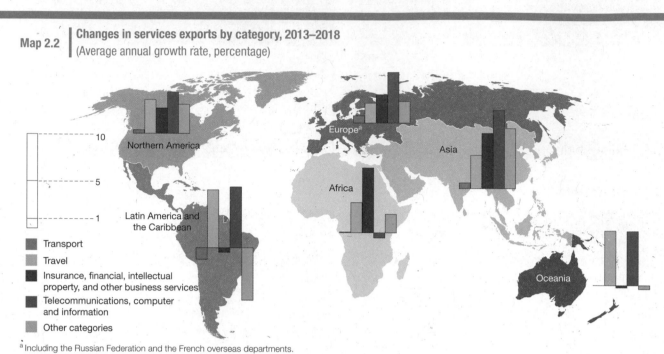

Transport
Travel
Insurance, financial, intellectual property, and other business services
Telecommunications, computer and information
Other categories

a Including the Russian Federation and the French overseas departments.

Concepts and definitions

The breakdown by service category in this section has been built from the division of services in the balance of payments statistics, known as the 2010 Extended Balance of Payments Services Classification (EBOPS 2010) (United Nations et al., 2012). For the correspondence to the EBOPS 2010 categories and to the main groups presented in UNCTADstat, see annex 6.2.

The presented trade-in-services figures are jointly compiled by UNCTAD, WTO and ITC.

Regional trends over five years

Between 2013 and 2018, exports of all categories of services, except transport, recorded ample growth in most regions of the world. Exports of telecommunications, computer and information services increased in Asia on average by 9.5 per cent each year, in Latin America and the Caribbean, Europe and Oceania between 6 and 7 per cent, while they stagnated in Africa. Africa, in turn, together with Asia, saw comparatively strong growth in exports of insurance, financial, intellectual property and other business services, increasing at annual rates between 6 and 7 per cent. This is noteworthy, given the small size of that sector of Africa, both in relation to the world market and to Africa's total services exports. Exports of travel grew on all continents – most notably in Latin America and the Caribbean, where an annual increase of 6.3 per cent was recorded.

Figure 2.2.1 | **Annual growth rate of services exports, 2018**
(Percentage)

Global trends in 2018

At world level, from 2017 to 2018, telecommunications, computer, and information services were the category for which world services trade expanded fastest, recording an annual growth of 14.7 per cent; about double the rate of transport, travel, insurance, financial, intellectual property and other business services. Exports of other types of services – mainly comprising goods-related services, construction, personal, cultural and recreational services and certain government goods and services – increased by 9.1 per cent between 2017 and 2018.

Figure 2.2.2 | **Structure of services exports, 2018**
(Percentage)

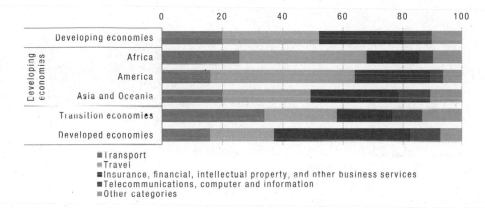

- ■ Transport
- ■ Travel
- ■ Insurance, financial, intellectual property, and other business services
- ■ Telecommunications, computer and information
- ■ Other categories

The structure of services exports today

In 2018, developing economies relied more on travel and transport and less on insurance, financial, intellectual property and other business services than developed economies for their exports. Those in America and Africa stood out with their relatively small share of telecommunications, computer and information services.

More than three quarters (78 per cent) of internationally traded insurance, financial, intellectual property and other business services were supplied by developed economies. Developing economies in Asia and Oceania accounted for slightly less than one fifth.

Figure 2.2.3 | **Exports of insurance, financial, intellectual property, and other business services, by group of economies, 2018**
(Percentage)

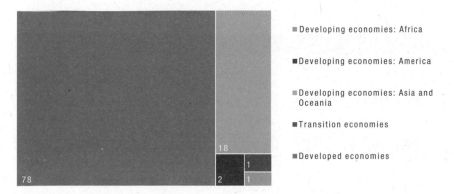

- ■ Developing economies: Africa
- ■ Developing economies: America
- ■ Developing economies: Asia and Oceania
- ■ Transition economies
- ■ Developed economies

Africa's exports of insurance, financial, IP, and other **business services grew** on average **6.4% each year** from 2013 to 2018

International trade in **telecommunications, computer, and information services** up by almost **15%** from 2017 to 2018

Transport and travel services **dominate** services **exports of developing** countries

78% of insurance, financial, IP, and other

business services exports **came from developed** economies in 2018

Table 2.2.1 | **Trade in services by service category and by group of economies**

Developing economies

Service category	Exports			Imports			Balance	
	Value		Annual growth rate	Value		Annual growth rate		
	(Billions of US$)		(Percentage)	(Billions of US$)		(Percentage)	(Billions of US$)	
	2013	2018	2018	2013	2018	2018	2013	2018
Total services	**1 394**	**1 738**	**9.3**	**1 745**	**2 118**	**8.1**	**-352**	**-380**
Transport	306	346	8.4	573	579	9.6	-267	-232
Travel	473	559	7.2	423	648	6.7	50	-89
Others	615	833	11.1	749	892	8.1	-135	-59

Developing economies: Africa

Service category	Exports			Imports			Balance	
	Value		Annual growth rate	Value		Annual growth rate		
	(Billions of US$)		(Percentage)	(Billions of US$)		(Percentage)	(Billions of US$)	
	2013	2018	2018	2013	2018	2018	2013	2018
Total services	**99**	**118**	**9.4**	**177**	**178**	**11.9**	**-77**	**-60**
Transport	28	30	8.2	69	66	12.7	-41	-36
Travel	40	50	12.5	25	29	19.6	15	21
Others	31	38	6.4	82	82	8.7	-52	-44

Developing economies: America

Service category	Exports			Imports			Balance	
	Value		Annual growth rate	Value		Annual growth rate		
	(Billions of US$)		(Percentage)	(Billions of US$)		(Percentage)	(Billions of US$)	
	2013	2018	2018	2013	2018	2018	2013	2018
Total services	**170**	**190**	**1.7**	**236**	**222**	**0.9**	**-67**	**-32**
Transport	32	30	3.1	70	63	5.1	-38	-33
Travel	67	91	3.8	59	61	-0.5	9	30
Others	71	69	-1.6	108	98	-0.9	-37	-29

Developing economies: Asia and Oceania

Service category	Exports			Imports			Balance	
	Value		Annual growth rate	Value		Annual growth rate		
	(Billions of US$)		(Percentage)	(Billions of US$)		(Percentage)	(Billions of US$)	
	2013	2018	2018	2013	2018	2018	2013	2018
Total services	**1 125**	**1 430**	**10.4**	**1 333**	**1 718**	**8.7**	**-207**	**-288**
Transport	246	286	9.0	434	449	9.8	-188	-164
Travel	365	418	7.3	339	557	7.0	26	-140
Others	514	726	12.7	559	711	9.4	-46	15

Transition economies

Service category	Exports			Imports			Balance	
	Value		Annual growth rate	Value		Annual growth rate		
	(Billions of US$)		(Percentage)	(Billions of US$)		(Percentage)	(Billions of US$)	
	2013	2018	2018	2013	2018	2018	2013	2018
Total services	**137**	**137**	**12.4**	**194**	**158**	**7.8**	**-57**	**-21**
Transport	45	46	11.1	34	31	10.6	11	16
Travel	32	33	14.7	73	56	9.2	-41	-23
Others	60	58	12.1	87	71	5.5	-26	-14

Developed economies

Service category	Exports			Imports			Balance	
	Value		Annual growth rate	Value		Annual growth rate		
	(Billions of US$)		(Percentage)	(Billions of US$)		(Percentage)	(Billions of US$)	
	2013	2018	2018	2013	2018	2018	2013	2018
Total services	**3 310**	**3 970**	**6.8**	**2 787**	**3 327**	**7.0**	**523**	**642**
Transport	590	624	6.4	571	606	8.1	19	18
Travel	693	844	7.0	605	701	7.7	89	144
Others	2 026	2 501	6.8	1 612	2 021	6.4	415	480

Table 2.2.2 | **Developing economies' exports of selected services by region, 2018**
(Millions of United States dollars)

Group of economies	Insurance and pension services	Financial services	Charges for the use of intellectual property n.i.e.	Telecommunications, computer, and information services	Other business services
World	**143 940**	**489 890**	**403 520**	**606 060**	**1 265 370**
Northern America	20 000	121 610	135 250	53 060	187 830
Latin America and the Caribbean	5 940	(e) 4 670	1 410	8 880	35 730
Europe	83 490	269 350	188 290	356 430	673 450
Sub-Saharan Africa	1 030	2 580	270	3 190	11 160
Western Asia and Northern Africa	10 770	5 670	5 710	30 680	28 450
Central and Southern Asia	3 010	6 340	960	62 360	70 150
Eastern and South-Eastern Asia	18 070	75 360	70 300	87 440	249 240
Oceania	720	4 300	1 330	4 010	9 350
Selected groups					
Developing economies excluding China	31 330	78 390	25 470	125 460	264 220
Developing economies excluding LDCs	36 000	81 410	30 950	169 950	330 040
LDCs	250	460	80	2 570	4 070
LLDCs	410	-	-	2 840	-
SIDS (UNCTAD)	490	230	30	530	1 610
HIPCs (IMF)	340	430	-	2 130	7 970
BRICS	8 730	12 140	8 170	113 690	165 720
G20	112 520	394 990	358 900	511 070	1 060 870

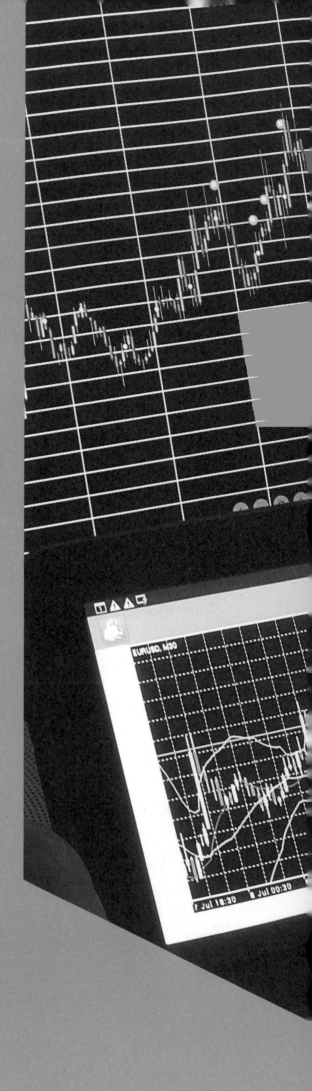

3

Economic trends

KEY FIGURES **2018**

Growth of world
real GDP per capita

+1.8%

FDI inflows to LDCs

US$24 billion

Change in
free market
commodity prices

+16%

NOWCAST **2019**

World real GDP
growth

+2.3%

3.1 Gross domestic product

Map 3.1 | **Gross domestic product per capita, 2018**
(United States dollars)

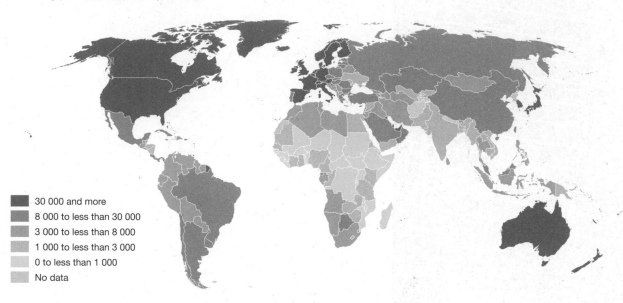

- 30 000 and more
- 8 000 to less than 30 000
- 3 000 to less than 8 000
- 1 000 to less than 3 000
- 0 to less than 1 000
- No data

Concepts and definitions

GDP is an aggregate measure of production, income and expenditure of an economy. As production measure, it represents the gross value added, i.e. the output net of intermediate consumption, achieved by all resident units engaged in production, plus any taxes less subsidies on products not included in the value of output. As income measure, it represents the sum of primary incomes (gross wages and entrepreneurial income) distributed by resident producers, plus taxes and less subsidies on production and imports. As expenditure measure, it depicts the sum of expenditure on final consumption, gross capital formation (i.e. investment, changes in inventories, and acquisitions less disposals of valuables) and exports after deduction of imports (United Nations et al., 2009).

The GDP figures presented in this section are calculated from the expenditure side.

Trends in global economy

In 2018, world real GDP grew by 3.0 per cent, almost at the same pace as in 2017 (3.1 per cent). In 2019, the GDP growth rate is nowcast at 2.3 per cent. This would be the lowest annual growth rate recorded since 2009.

Large differences in GDP per capita persist throughout the world. In 2018, most developed economies produced an output per person greater than US$30 000, with economies in Eastern Europe as the main exception. By contrast, almost half of the developing economies in Africa – all of them least developed countries (LDCs) – recorded a per capita output of less than US$1 000. Most developing economies in America, Western, Central and Eastern Asia and in Oceania reached an output higher than US$3 000 per person.

Figure 3.1.1 | **World real gross domestic product annual growth rate**
(Percentage)

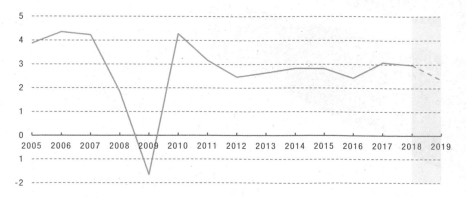

Note: At constant 2010 United States dollars. The shaded area indicates UNCTAD nowcasts. For the methodology, see annex 6.3.

Regional trends

Not all regions of the world recorded equal economic growth in 2018. Growth remained high, at 5.3 per cent, in developing Asia and Oceania, whereas in the developing economies of America GDP increased by only 0.7 per cent. The growth rate of transition and developed economies stood at 2.8 and 2.2 per cent, respectively.

GDP in LDCs grew at a higher rate than the world average in 2018, as in the previous year, but at 4.7 per cent their growth rate remained below the 7 per cent target set by the 2030 Agenda for Sustainable Development. GDP per capita increased by 2.3 per cent in LDCs.

World economy grew steadily – at 3% in 2018

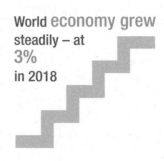

Figure 3.1.2 | Growth of real gross domestic product by group of economies, 2018
(Percentage)

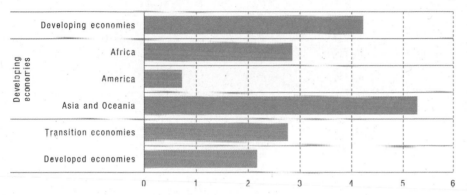

Note. At constant 2010 United States dollars.

Global economic inequality

Over the last ten years, the global distribution of nominal GDP per capita between economies has become more equal. For example, in 2008, the poorest economies, accounting for 80 per cent of the world's population, contributed 23 per cent to world GDP. By 2018, their share in GDP rose to 33 per cent. Between 2013 and 2018, however, inequalities in GDP per capita reduced mainly among economies with moderately high income. The relative distance between the richest and poorest economies in the world remained almost unchanged.

 5.3% GDP growth in developing economies of Asia and Oceania

Growth rate of LDCs still below 2030 Agenda target of 7%

Figure 3.1.3 | Distribution of world gross domestic product
(Percentage)

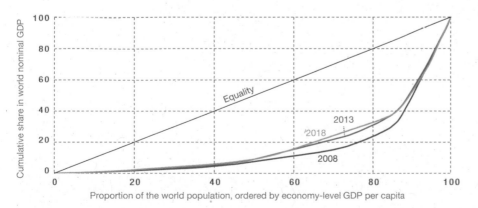

Proportion of the world population, ordered by economy-level GDP per capita

Note: Lorenz curves, as in this graph, reveal the structure of inequality. Inequality is greater the further the curve runs below the diagonal line (see annex 6.3). Inequality within economies is not considered.

The 20% in the richest economies accounted for 66% of world GDP in 2018

Table 3.1.1 | Gross domestic product and gross domestic product per capita

Group of economies	Value		Annual growth rate			
	Nominal GDP	Nominal GDP per capita	Real GDP[a]		Real GDP[a] per capita	
	(Billions of US$)	(US$)	(Percentage)		(Percentage)	
	2018	2018	2017	2018	2017	2018
World	**85 304**	**11 181**	**3.1**	**3.0**	**1.9**	**1.8**
Developing economies	33 829	5 405	4.4	4.2	3.1	2.9
Developing economies: Africa	2 359	1 851	2.9	2.9	0.3	0.3
Developing economies: America	5 454	8 553	0.8	0.7	-0.1	-0.2
Developing economies: Asia and Oceania	26 016	5 985	5.5	5.3	4.5	4.3
Transition economies	2 274	7 332	2.1	2.8	1.7	2.4
Developed economies	49 200	46 378	2.3	2.2	1.9	1.8
Selected groups						
Developing economies excluding China	20 224	4 186	3.2	3.0	1.6	1.5
Developing economies excluding LDCs	32 758	6 241	4.4	4.2	3.3	3.1
LDCs	1 071	1 061	4.5	4.7	2.1	2.3
LLDCs	782	1 537	4.5	4.6	2.0	2.1
SIDS (UNCTAD)	101	7 855	0.9	2.4	-0.2	1.3
HIPCs (IMF)	680	944	5.4	5.1	2.5	2.2
BRICS	20 218	6 331	5.3	5.4	4.5	4.7
G20	73 602	15 232	3.1	3.0	2.4	2.3

[a] At constant 2010 United States dollars.

Table 3.1.2 | Nominal gross domestic product by type of expenditure, 2017
(Percentage)

Group of economies	Final consumption		Gross capital formation	Net exports of goods and services
	Households[a]	Government[b]		
World	**56.9**	**16.2**	**25.7**	**0.8**
Developing economies	51.1	14.4	32.2	1.1
Developing economies: Africa	66.7	14.1	23.6	-5.0
Developing economies: America	65.4	16.5	18.8	-0.9
Developing economies: Asia and Oceania	46.3	13.9	36.2	2.2
Transition economies	53.7	17.1	24.9	3.8
Developed economies	60.9	17.4	21.3	0.4
Selected groups				
Developing economies excluding China	59.1	14.5	25.1	0.7
Developing economies excluding LDCs	50.5	14.5	32.4	1.5
LDCs	68.4	10.4	27.9	-8.6
LLDCs	60.8	13.4	28.7	-4.1
SIDS (UNCTAD)	67.8	15.8	20.7	-5.9
HIPCs (IMF)	69.7	12.9	26.2	-10.3
BRICS	45.5	14.9	36.7	1.3
G20	56.5	16.5	25.9	0.6

[a] Including non-profit institutions serving households.
[b] General government.

Table 3.1.3 | **Nominal gross value added by economic activity**
(Percentage)

Group of economies	Agriculture		Industry		Services	
	2007	2017	2007	2017	2007	2017
World	**3.5**	**4.3**	**29.5**	**28.1**	**67.0**	**67.5**
Developing economies	8.9	8.7	38.9	35.8	52.2	55.5
Developing economies: Africa	15.0	16.9	35.0	29.5	50.0	53.6
Developing economies: America	5.3	5.5	33.1	27.9	61.7	66.7
Developing economies: Asia and Oceania	9.2	8.7	41.6	38.1	49.2	53.3
Transition economies	5.9	5.8	36.8	33.8	57.4	60.4
Developed economies	1.4	1.3	25.5	22.7	73.2	76.1
Selected groups						
Developing economies excluding China	8.3	8.9	36.4	32.1	55.2	58.9
Developing economies excluding LDCs	8.4	8.2	39.2	36.0	52.4	55.8
LDCs	24.0	22.1	31.0	29.3	45.0	48.6
LLDCs	17.4	16.8	35.6	32.2	47.0	51.0
SIDS (UNCTAD)	4.2	5.0	32.2	24.6	63.6	70.4
HIPCs (IMF)	24.7	24.5	27.2	27.8	48.2	47.6
BRICS	9.6	8.8	39.5	37.0	50.9	54.3
G20	2.9	3.7	28.4	27.6	68.7	68.7

Table 3.1.4 | **Economies with highest gross domestic product per capita**

Economy	Nominal value		Real annual growth rate[a]	Structure by type of expenditure			
				Final consumption		Gross capital formation	Net exports of goods and services
				Household[b]	Government[c]		
	(US$)		(Percentage)	(Percentage)	(Percentage)	(Percentage)	(Percentage)
	2017	2018	2018	2017	2017	2017	2017
Luxembourg	105 279	113 314	0.5	30.7	17.0	19.0	33.3
Bermuda	99 451	102 987	1.8	51.4	16.0	13.7	19.4
China, Macao SAR	80 891	86 914	4.3	24.2	9.9	18.5	47.4
Switzerland, Liechtenstein	80 676	82 904	1.7	53.8	12.0	23.5	10.7
Norway	75 424	81 477	0.6	44.5	24.1	28.2	3.2
Ireland	69 727	77 307	5.3	31.9	12.1	24.7	30.4
Iceland	73 198	76 809	3.9	50.3	23.3	22.3	4.1
Qatar	61 513	68 932	-0.7	24.7	22.4	39.3	13.7
Cayman Islands	63 589	66 980	1.9	63.4	14.6	22.4	0.7
United States of America	59 660	62 380	2.3	68.3	14.0	20.5	-2.8

[a] At constant 2010 United States dollars.
[b] Including non-profit institutions serving households.
[c] General government.
Note: Economies are ranked by the nominal value in 2018.

3.2 Current account

Map 3.2 | **Current account balance as a ratio to gross domestic product, 2018**
(Percentage)

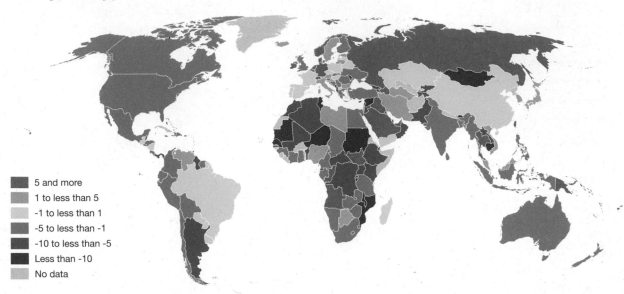

5 and more
1 to less than 5
-1 to less than 1
-5 to less than -1
-10 to less than -5
Less than -10
No data

Concepts and definitions

The current account, within the balance of payments, displays the transactions between residents and non-residents of a reporting economy, involving economic values, namely the cross-national exchange of goods and services as well as cross-national transfers of primary and secondary income.

The current account balance shows the difference between the sum of exports and income receivable and the sum of imports and income payable, where exports and imports refer to both goods and services, while income refers to both primary and secondary income. A surplus in the current account is recorded when receipts exceed expenditures; a deficit is recorded when expenditures exceed receipts.

The current account data in this section correspond to the latest reporting standard, known as BPM6, defined by the International Monetary Fund (2009).

Geographic distribution of current account imbalances

Receipts earned by economies from transactions with other economies often differ significantly from payments made. In 2018, for most economies in America, Africa, Southern and South-Eastern Asia and Oceania payments exceeded receipts, leading to negative current account balances. High surpluses were found mainly in petroleum exporting economies. The accounts of European and Eastern Asian economies were generally more balanced.

Figure 3.2.1 | **Balances in the current account**
(Billions of United States dollars)

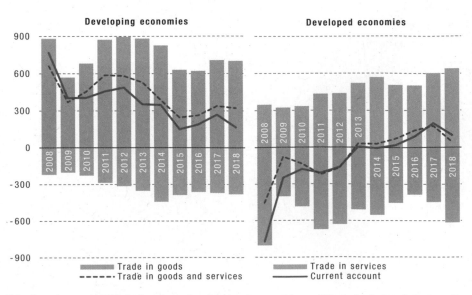

Note: Current account deficits and surpluses do not add up to zero at the world level, due to imperfect geographic coverage and cross-country differences in compilation methods.

In two island economies of the Caribbean, Dominica (47 per cent) and Anguilla (45 per cent), current account deficits were almost half the value of GDP. High deficits relative to GDP were also recorded in Mozambique (30 per cent), Lebanon (27 per cent) and the Maldives (26 per cent). In absolute terms, the United States of America (US$490 billion) ran the world's largest current account deficit. Germany (US$291 billion) had the largest surplus, in absolute terms.

Recent developments

In 2018, the current account surplus for developing economies dropped to US$167 billion, by more than one third compared with 2017. This was driven mainly by falling incomes and current transfers, and less by developments in international trade. The decline can largely be attributed to a drop in current account balances (from US$418 billion to US$342 billion) in Asian developing economies, combined with slightly rising deficits in African and American developing economies.

The current account surplus in developed economies, which had emerged in 2015, stood at US$99 billion in 2018; half of the amount recorded in 2017. This decrease was driven by increasing imports of goods, relative to exports.

Figure 3.2.2 | **Balances in least developed countries' current accounts**
(Billions of United States dollars)

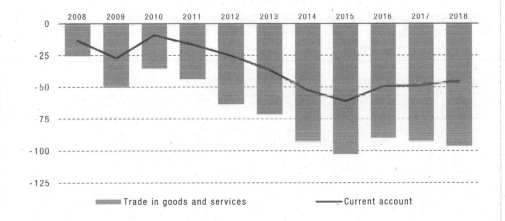

Trade in goods and services   Current account

The least developed countries' persistent deficit

After five years of continuous decline, from 2011 to 2015, the current account balance of LDCs improved in 2016. Since then, their deficit has remained at just below US$50 billion, despite a slight decrease of their trade balance.

The high relative current account deficit, accounting for 4.2 per cent of GDP in 2018, distinguishes LDCs from other developing economies, which, as a group, ran a surplus of 0.5 per cent of GDP. Higher deficits relative to GDP were registered also for other groups of vulnerable economies, such as heavily indebted poor countries (HIPCs) (5.2 per cent) and small island developing States (SIDS) (4.7 per cent). In landlocked developing countries (LLDCs), the deficit stood at 2.8 per cent of GDP.

Current account deficits of Dominica and Anguilla:
almost $\frac{1}{2}$ of GDP

United States of America had world's largest deficit:

US$490 billion

Developing economies' surplus down by $\frac{1}{3}$

Deficit in SIDS
4.7% of GDP

Table 3.2.1 | Current account balance by group of economies

Group of economies	Value (Billions of US$)			Ratio to GDP (Percentage)		
	2014–2018[a]	2017	2018	2014–2018[a]	2017	2018
Developing economies	225	269	167	0.7	0.8	0.5
Developing economies: Africa	-109	-73	-77	-4.7	-3.3	-3.3
Developing economies: America	-124	-77	-98	-2.2	-1.3	-1.8
Developing economies: Asia and Oceania	458	418	342	2.0	1.7	1.3
Transition economies	43	15	103	1.9	0.7	4.5
Developed economies	81	197	100	0.2	0.4	0.2
Selected groups						
Developing economies excluding China	28	74	118	0.1	0.4	0.6
Developing economies excluding LDCs	277	317	212	0.9	1.0	0.7
LDCs	-51	-49	-45	-5.2	-4.5	-4.2
LLDCs	-29	-30	-22	-4.0	-4.2	-2.8
SIDS (UNCTAD)	-3	-5	-5	-3.5	-4.8	-4.7
HIPCs (IMF)	-42	-34	-35	-7.1	-5.5	-5.2
BRICS	170	173	69	1.0	0.9	0.3
G20	147	268	97	0.2	0.4	0.1

Note: Current account deficits and surpluses do not add up to zero across groups of economies, due to imperfect geographic coverage and cross-country differences in compilation methods.
[a] Annual average.

Table 3.2.2 | Current account balance in largest surplus and deficit economies

Economy (Ranked by 2018 value)	2014–2018[a] Value (Billions of US$)	2014–2018[a] Ratio to GDP (Percentage)	2017 Value (Billions of US$)	2017 Ratio to GDP (Percentage)	2018 Value (Billions of US$)	2018 Ratio to GDP (Percentage)
Germany	289	7.9	296	8.0	291	7.3
Japan	149	3.1	202	4.1	175	3.5
Russian Federation	59	3.7	32	2.1	113	7.0
Netherlands	75	8.9	90	10.9	99	10.8
Korea, Republic of	88	6.0	75	4.9	76	4.7
⋮	⋮	⋮	⋮	⋮	⋮	⋮
Indonesia	-22	-2.3	-16	-1.6	-31	-3.0
Canada	-48	-2.9	-46	-2.8	-45	-2.7
India	-33	-1.4	-38	-1.5	-66	-2.4
United Kingdom	-126	-4.5	-88	-3.3	-109	-3.9
United States of America	-426	-2.2	-440	-2.2	-491	-2.4

[a] Annual average.

Table 3.2.3 | Current accounts of leading exporters (goods and services) by group of economies, 2018

Developing economies: Africa

Economy (Ranked by export share)	Current account balance Value (Billions of US$)	Current account balance Ratio to GDP (Percentage)	Trade balance[a] Value (Billions of US$)	Exports[a] Share in world (Percentage)	Imports[a] Share in world (Percentage)
South Africa	-13	-3.6	1	0.4	0.4
Nigeria	5	1.3	(e) -4	(e) 0.3	(e) 0.3
Egypt	-6	-2.5	(e) -25	(e) 0.2	(e) 0.3
Algeria	(e) -16	(e) -9.1	(e) -13	(e) 0.2	(e) 0.2
Morocco	-6	-5.5	-12	0.2	0.2
Developing Africa	**-77**	**-3.3**	**-102**	**2.4**	**2.9**

[a] Goods and services.

Developing economies: America

Economy (Ranked by export share)	Current account balance		Trade balance[a]	Exports[a]	Imports[a]
	Value	Ratio to GDP	Value	Share in world	Share in world
	(Billions of US$)	(Percentage)	(Billions of US$)	(Percentage)	(Percentage)
Mexico	-22	-1.8	(e) -22	(e) 1.9	(e) 2.1
Brazil	-15	-0.8	20	1.1	1.0
Chile	-9	-3.1	(e) 1	(e) 0.3	(e) 0.3
Argentina	-27	-5.3	-11	0.3	0.4
Peru	-4	-1.6	(e) 5	(e) 0.2	(e) 0.2
Developing America	**-98**	**-1.8**	**-39**	**5.1**	**5.4**

[a] Goods and services.

Developing economies: Asia and Oceania

Economy (Ranked by export share)	Current account balance		Trade balance[a]	Exports[a]	Imports[a]
	Value	Ratio to GDP	Value	Share in world	Share in world
	(Billions of US$)	(Percentage)	(Billions of US$)	(Percentage)	(Percentage)
China	49	0.4	137	10.7	10.4
Korea, Republic of	76	4.7	(e) 84	(e) 2.9	(e) 2.6
China, Hong Kong SAR	16	4.3	(e) 0	(e) 2.7	(e) 2.8
Singapore	65	10.7	95	2.5	2.2
India	-66	-2.4	(e) -159	(e) 2.2	(e) 2.8
Developing Asia and Oceania	**342**	**1.3**	**464**	**34.0**	**32.8**

[a] Goods and services.

Transition economies

Economy (Ranked by export share)	Current account balance		Trade balance[a]	Exports[a]	Imports[a]
	Value	Ratio to GDP	Value	Share in world	Share in world
	(Billions of US$)	(Percentage)	(Billions of US$)	(Percentage)	(Percentage)
Russian Federation	113	7.0	(e) 165	(e) 2.0	(e) 1.4
Kazakhstan	0	0.0	22	0.3	0.2
Ukraine	-4	-3.4	-11	0.2	0.3
Belarus	0	-0.4	1	0.2	0.2
Serbia	-3	-4.7	-4	0.1	0.1
Transition economies	**103**	**4.5**	**162**	**3.2**	**2.6**

[a] Goods and services.

Developed economies

Economy (Ranked by export share)	Current account balance		Trade balance[a]	Exports[a]	Imports[a]
	Value	Ratio to GDP	Value	Share in world	Share in world
	(Billions of US$)	(Percentage)	(Billions of US$)	(Percentage)	(Percentage)
United States of America	-491	-2.4	(e) -618	(e) 10.0	(e) 12.8
Germany	291	7.3	(e) 242	(e) 7.4	(e) 6.6
Japan	175	3.5	(e) 3	(e) 3.7	(e) 3.8
France	-18	-0.6	(e) -21	(e) 3.6	(e) 3.8
United Kingdom	-109	-3.9	(e) -43	(e) 3.4	(e) 3.6
Developed economies	**100**	**0.2**	**46**	**55.3**	**56.3**

[a] Goods and services.

3.3 Foreign direct investment

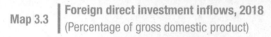

Map 3.3 | **Foreign direct investment inflows, 2018**
(Percentage of gross domestic product)

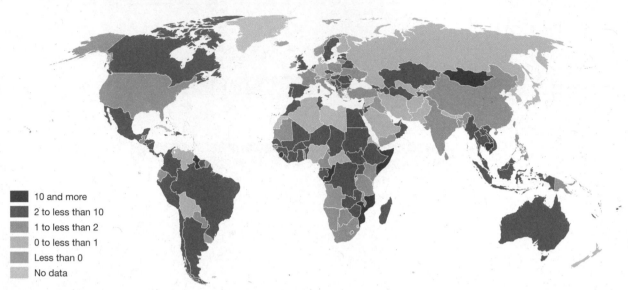

- 10 and more
- 2 to less than 10
- 1 to less than 2
- 0 to less than 1
- Less than 0
- No data

Concepts and definitions

Foreign direct investment (FDI) is defined as an investment reflecting a lasting interest and control by a foreign direct investor, resident in one economy, in an enterprise resident in another economy (foreign affiliate).

FDI inflows comprise capital provided by a foreign direct investor to a foreign affiliate, or capital received by a foreign direct investor from a foreign affiliate. FDI outflows represent the same flows from the perspective of the other economy.

FDI flows are presented on a net basis, i.e. as credits less debits. Thus, in cases of reverse investment or disinvestment, FDI may be negative.

FDI stock is the value of capital and reserves attributable to a non-resident parent enterprise, plus the net indebtedness of foreign affiliates to parent enterprises (UNCTAD, 2019b).

Trends and global patterns

In 2018, world FDI inflows decreased by 13 per cent to US$1.3 trillion. This is the third consecutive annual decline. FDI to developed economies fell to US$557 billion, whereas flows to developing economies remained stable at around US$700 billion. As a result, unlike previous years, more FDI was directed to developing than to developed economies (this excludes financial centers in the Caribbean characterized by atypical use of FDI and difficulties in measurement).

In 2018, eight of the top 20 host economies were developing economies. But the largest recipient of FDI was the United States of America, followed by China, Hong Kong SAR and Singapore. For most countries in Latin America and the Caribbean, Africa and South-Eastern Asia, FDI inflows accounted for more than two per cent of national GDP. The world's largest foreign direct investors were Japan, China and France.

Figure 3.3.1 | **World foreign direct investment inflows**
(Billions of United States dollars)

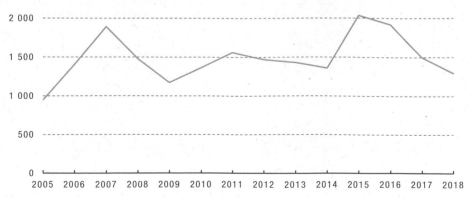

Note: Excluding financial centres in the Caribbean (see note, table 3.3.1).

Inflows and outflows by group of economies

In 2018, FDI inflows to developing economies amounted to US$706 billion, three quarter more than their FDI outflows (US$418 billion). 73 per cent of these inflows and 96 per cent of the outflows were attributed to developing economies in Asia and Oceania. Developing economies in America and Africa attracted less FDI and played only a marginal role as foreign direct investors. Developed and transition economies generated as much FDI as they received.

Figure 3.3.2 | **Foreign direct investment inflows and outflows, 2018**
(Billions of United States dollars)

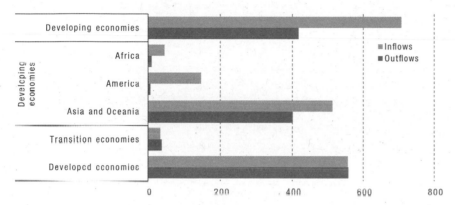

Note: Excluding financial centres in the Caribbean (see note, table 3.3.1).

Origins and destinations of foreign direct investment

Between 2017 and 2018, developed economies' share of global outward FDI dropped from 65 to 55 per cent. This was mainly due to a drastic fall of FDI from American developed economies from 27 per cent to less than zero in 2018, reflecting a net disinvestment equivalent to 1 per cent of world FDI. On the recipient side, the relative importance of the developing world as a host region increased, but mainly as a result of the negative trend in developed economies. Asia and Oceania strengthened their position within the developing world, accounting for 40 per cent of world FDI in 2018.[1]

[1] For further analyses on that topic, see UNCTAD (2019b).

Figure 3.3.3 | **Selected foreign direct investment flows**
(Percentage of world total)

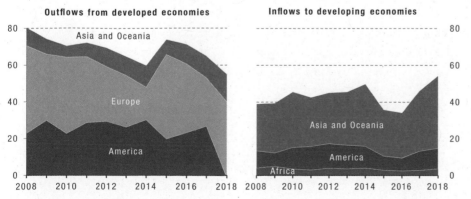

Note: Excluding financial centres in the Caribbean (see note, table 3.3.1).

Global **FDI** dropped by 13% in 2018

Developing economies **receive almost twice** as much FDI as they initiate

FDI from **Northern America** slumped

Developing Asia and Oceania now account for **40%** of world **FDI inflows**

Table 3.3.1 | Foreign direct investment flows by group of economies

Group of economies	Inflows				Outflows			
	Value (Billions of US$)		Ratio to GDP (Percentage)		Value (Billions of US$)		Ratio to GDP (Percentage)	
	2013	2018	2013	2018	2013	2018	2013	2018
World	**1 431**	**1 297**	**1.9**	**1.5**	**1 377**	**1 014**	**1.8**	**1.2**
Developing economies	653	706	2.3	2.1	409	418	1.5	1.3
Developing economies: Africa	50	46	2.1	2.0	11	10	0.5	0.5
Developing economies: America	184	147	3.0	2.8	35	7	0.6	0.1
Developing economies: Asia and Oceania	418	513	2.1	2.0	363	401	1.8	1.6
Transition economies	84	34	2.7	1.5	76	38	2.5	1.7
Developed economies	695	557	1.5	1.1	892	558	2.0	1.1
Selected groups								
Developing economies excluding China	529	567	2.8	2.8	301	288	1.6	1.5
Developing economies excluding LDCs	632	682	2.3	2.1	406	417	1.5	1.3
LDCs	21	24	2.4	2.2	3	1	0.5	0.1
LLDCs	30	23	3.7	2.9	4	1	0.8	0.2
SIDS (UNCTAD)	1	2	1.0	2.6	0	0	0.3	0.4
HIPCs (IMF)	30	27	5.4	4.0	2	1	0.5	0.3
BRICS	273	261	1.6	1.3	186	169	1.1	0.8
G20	1 060	997	1.6	1.4	1 086	774	1.6	1.1

Note: Excluding financial centres in the Caribbean, namely: Anguilla, Antigua and Barbuda, Aruba, the Bahamas, Barbados, British Virgin Islands, Cayman Islands, Curaçao, Dominica, Grenada, Montserrat, Saint Kitts and Nevis, Saint Lucia, Saint Vincent and the Grenadines, Sint Maarten and Turks and Caicos Islands.

Table 3.3.2 | Foreign direct investment stock by group of economies

Group of economies	Inward stock				Outward stock			
	Value (Billions of US$)		Ratio to GDP (Percentage)		Value (Billions of US$)		Ratio to GDP (Percentage)	
	2013	2018	2013	2018	2013	2018	2013	2018
World	**24 671**	**32 272**	**32**	**38**	**24 832**	**30 975**	**32**	**37**
Developing economies	7 780	10 679	27	32	4 408	7 524	16	23
Developing economies: Africa	723	895	30	38	189	318	8	15
Developing economies: America	1 858	2 116	30	40	572	659	10	13
Developing economies: Asia and Oceania	5 199	7 668	26	29	3 648	6 547	18	25
Transition economies	809	804	26	35	432	402	14	18
Developed economies	16 081	20 790	36	42	19 991	23 049	44	47
Selected groups								
Developing economies excluding China	6 824	9 051	36	45	3 748	5 585	20	29
Developing economies excluding LDCs	7 546	10 325	27	32	4 392	7 502	16	23
LDCs	234	354	27	33	16	22	3	3
LLDCs	284	391	36	51	39	48	7	9
SIDS (UNCTAD)	40	48	54	63	3	3	4	4
HIPCs (IMF)	202	331	36	49	15	21	3	4
BRICS	2 435	3 234	15	16	1 498	2 916	9	14
G20	18 679	23 985	28	33	20 512	25 189	31	34

Note: Excluding financial centres in the Caribbean (see note, table 3.3.1).

Table 3.3.3 | Foreign direct investment inflows, top 20 host economies, 2018

Economy (Ranked by inflow value)	Inflows		Inward stock
	Value	**Ratio to GDP**	**Ratio to GDP**
	(Billions of US$)	(Percentage)	(Percentage)
United States of America	252	1.2	36
China	139	1.0	12
China, Hong Kong SAR	116	31.9	550
Singapore	78	22.4	426
Netherlands	70	7.6	183
United Kingdom	64	2.3	67
Brazil	61	3.3	37
Australia	60	4.2	47
Spain	44	3.1	46
India	42	1.5	14
Canada	40	2.3	52
France	37	1.3	30
Mexico	32	2.6	40
Germany	26	0.6	24
Italy	24	1.2	21
Indonesia	22	2.1	22
Israel	22	5.9	40
Viet Nam	16	6.3	59
Korea, Republic of	14	0.9	14
Russian Federation	13	0.8	25

Note: Excluding financial centres in the Caribbean (see note, table 3.3.1).

Table 3.3.4 | Foreign direct investment outflows, top 20 home economies, 2018

Economy (Ranked by outflow value)	Outflows		Outward stock
	Value	**Ratio to GDP**	**Ratio to GDP**
	(Billions of US$)	(Percentage)	(Percentage)
Japan	143	2.9	33
China	130	1.0	14
France	102	3.7	54
China, Hong Kong SAR	85	23.5	515
Germany	77	1.9	41
Netherlands	59	6.5	266
Canada	50	3.0	78
United Kingdom	50	1.8	60
Korea, Republic of	39	2.4	24
Singapore	37	10.7	294
Russian Federation	36	2.2	21
Spain	32	2.2	40
Switzerland, Liechtenstein	27	3.8	178
Saudi Arabia	21	2.7	14
Italy	21	1.0	26
Sweden	20	3.6	67
China, Taiwan Province of	18	3.1	58
Thailand	18	3.5	24
United Arab Emirates	15	3.6	33
Ireland	13	3.6	245

Note: Excluding financial centres in the Caribbean (see note, table 3.3.1).

3.4 Prices

Map 3.4 | **Annual growth of consumer prices, 2018**
(Percentage)

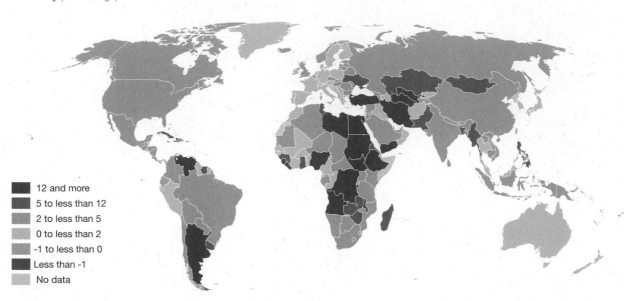

- 12 and more
- 5 to less than 12
- 2 to less than 5
- 0 to less than 2
- -1 to less than 0
- Less than -1
- No data

Concepts and definitions

Changes in consumer prices are measured by the consumer price index (CPI) that depicts the price of a basket of consumer goods and services, representing average consumption by private households during a year, relative to the base year 2010.

The UNCTAD free market commodity price index (FMCPI) measures the average price, in United States dollars, of main primary commodities exported by developing economies, relative to the base year 2015. The weights used in the calculation of the average price represent the shares of commodity groups in developing economies' total commodity exports, observed over three years from 2014 to 2016. The overall index is decomposed into sub-indices displaying the price movements of individual commodity groups. The basket of the FMCPI has been entirely overhauled in 2018. For details, see annex 6.3 and UNCTAD (2018).

Consumer prices and exchange rates

In 2018, consumer prices rose with different speeds throughout the world. Relatively high inflation rates were widespread in the central and north-eastern regions of Africa and in Central Asia, as well as in Argentina, Yemen, Iran and Turkey, and in Venezuela where consumer prices rocketed. In developed economies, consumer prices remained relatively stable. In most economies of Europe, in Israel, Japan, Australia and New Zealand they increased at a rate lower than 2 per cent. Several developing economies in Western Africa, South-Eastern Asia and Oceania recorded equally low inflation.

In 2018, for the first time since 2011, the four most traded currencies appreciated against the United States dollar. The value of the euro increased by 5 per cent, pound sterling by 4 per cent, and yuan and yen by 2 per cent.

Figure 3.4.1 | **Exchange rates against the United States dollar**
(Annual average)

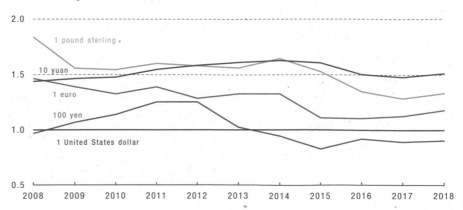

Commodity price index rising

In 2018, the FMCPI increased by 16 per cent compared with the previous year, indicating that prices of main commodities exported by developing economies continued their upward trend since 2016.

The main driver of the rise of the FMCPI in 2018 was fuels (+27.5 per cent). The index without fuels decreased slightly, by 1.5 per cent. Falling prices for food prices (-6.5 per cent), especially tropical beverages (-8.5 per cent), were the main factor behind that development.

Figure 3.4.2 | **Free market commodity price index**
(2015=100)

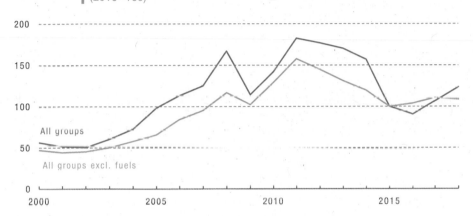

Inflation in many **African** economies among **the highest**

Trends of commodity prices in 2018 and 2019

Although fuel prices for 2018 as a whole increased by 27.6 per cent, in December 2018 they were almost the same as in December 2017. By May 2019, the trend had reversed, and fuel prices began steadily falling. In August, they were 22 per cent lower than the previous August 2018, suggesting that the annual increase of 2018 will be followed by a fall in 2019. Prices of agricultural raw materials in 2019 have also remained below their values of 12 months earlier. Until August that difference rose to 6 per cent.

By contrast, prices for minerals, ores and metals recovered in 2019 from a previous downturn. Between January and August, their year-on-year growth rate surged from -11 to +15 per cent. In July and August 2019, food prices returned, for the first time since mid-2017, to a positive annual trend.

The **pound sterling appreciated** against the United States dollar by **+4%**,

the **Euro** by **+5%**

Fuel prices up by **16%** in 2018,

but in **spring 2019** the **trend reversed**

Figure 3.4.3 | **Year-on-year growth of prices by commodity group**
(Percentage)

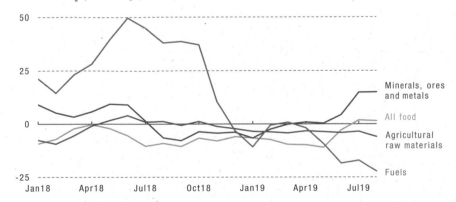

Note: Percentage change of FMCPI sub-indices, compared to the same month in the previous year.

Prices for **minerals, ores** and **metals** recovering – in August: **+15%** year-on-year

Table 3.4.1 | Consumer prices by group of economies

Group of economies	Consumer price index (2010=100)		Annual growth rate (Percentage)	
	2013	2018	2013–2018	2018
World	**110**	**126**	**2.6**	**3.2**
Developing economies	118	147	4.5	5.0
Developing economies: Africa	127	205	10.1	10.9
Developing economies: America	117	163	6.9	6.3
Developing economies: Asia and Oceania	117	137	3.2	4.0
Transition economies	124	182	8.0	4.1
Developed economies	106	112	1.2	1.9
Selected groups				
Developing economies excluding China	121	161	5.8	6.5
Developing economies excluding LDCs	118	145	4.3	4.7
LDCs	136	239	11.9	13.7
LLDCs	124	191	8.9	7.9
SIDS (UNCTAD)	118	133	2.5	2.4
HIPCs (IMF)	125	170	6.3	6.3
BRICS	117	140	3.7	2.8
G20	109	122	2.2	2.7

Note: Venezuela is not considered in the aggregations.

Table 3.4.2 | Exchange rate and consumer prices among main exporting economies

Economy (Ranked by share in world exports)	Exchange rate to United States dollar			Consumer price index (2010=100)			Share in world exports[a] (Percentage)
	2016	2017	2018	2016	2017	2018	2018
China	0.15050	0.14796	0.15115	117	119	122	10.7
United States of America	1.00000	1.00000	1.00000	110	112	115	(e) 10.0
Germany	1.10615	1.12689	1.18038	108	109	111	(e) 7.4
Japan	0.00919	0.00892	0.00906	103	104	105	(e) 3.7
France	1.10615	1.12689	1.18038	106	107	109	(e) 3.6
United Kingdom	1.35019	1.28700	1.33408	112	115	118	(e) 3.4
Netherlands	1.10615	1.12689	1.18038	110	111	113	(e) 3.3
Korea, Republic of	0.00086	0.00088	0.00091	111	113	115	(e) 2.9
China, Hong Kong SAR	0.12883	0.12832	0.12758	126	128	131	(e) 2.7
Italy	1.10615	1.12689	1.18038	107	109	110	(e) 2.6
Singapore	0.72383	0.72415	0.74138	113	113	114	2.5
Canada	0.75437	0.77045	0.77173	110	112	115	(e) 2.2
India	0.01488	0.01536	0.01462	156	160	168	(e) 2.2
Russian Federation	0.01491	0.01714	0.01596	162	168	173	(e) 2.0
Spain	1.10615	1.12689	1.18038	106	108	110	(e) 2.0
Mexico	0.05358	0.05284	0.05196	123	130	137	(e) 1.9
Belgium	1.10615	1.12689	1.18038	111	113	115	(e) 1.9
Switzerland, Liechtenstein	1.01482	1.01555	1.02262	98	98	99	1.8
Ireland	1.10615	1.12689	1.18038	105	105	106	(e) 1.8
China, Taiwan Province of	0.03094	0.03285	0.03315	106	107	109	(e) 1.6

[a] Exports of goods and services.

Table 3.4.3 | **Indices of free market prices of selected primary commodities**
(2015=100)

Commodity group	2010	2011	2012	2013	2014	2015	2016	2017	2018
All groups	**142**	**182**	**177**	**170**	**157**	**100**	**91**	**106**	**123**
All food	114	141	132	120	119	100	104	102	96
Food	111	135	127	120	118	100	104	103	96
Tropical beverages	110	144	112	90	111	100	97	94	86
Vegetable oilseeds and oils	121	151	152	136	123	100	107	106	100
Agricultural raw materials	142	177	143	131	115	100	100	105	103
Minerals, ores and metals	136	164	153	138	121	100	105	116	118
Minerals, ores and non-precious metals	170	191	159	156	133	100	101	128	131
Precious metals	110	143	148	125	111	100	107	108	108
Fuels	150	198	197	194	180	100	83	104	132
Selected groups									
Tropical beverages and food	111	137	124	112	117	100	102	101	94
All groups excl. fuels	129	158	145	131	119	100	104	110	109
All groups excl. precious metals	146	188	181	176	163	100	88	106	126
All groups excl. precious metals and fuels	138	164	143	134	123	100	102	112	109

Table 3.4.4 | **Monthly indices of free market prices by main commodity group**
(2015=100)

	Period	All groups	All food	Agricultural raw materials	Minerals, ores and metals	Fuels
2018	January	**123**	99	105	125	129
	February	**118**	100	105	125	121
	March	**119**	102	106	122	122
	April	**124**	102	105	121	130
	May	**128**	101	105	121	138
	June	**127**	96	104	121	137
	July	**125**	92	102	114	136
	August	**124**	91	103	112	135
	September	**130**	89	102	111	146
	October	**132**	92	101	114	149
	November	**120**	91	99	114	129
	December	**111**	92	100	114	115
2019	January	**112**	93	101	116	115
	February	**116**	93	101	122	120
	March	**118**	92	101	121	123
	April	**121**	92	102	122	128
	May	**119**	90	101	121	125
	June	**112**	94	100	126	112
	July	**114**	94	99	131	113
	August	**109**	92	97	129	106

4

Population

KEY FIGURES **2018**

World population
7.6 billion

Annual
population growth
+1.1%

Share of urban
population in
developing economies
51%

Child dependency
ratio in LDCs
69%

4.1 Total and urban population

Map 4.1 | **Annual population growth, 2018**
(Percentage)

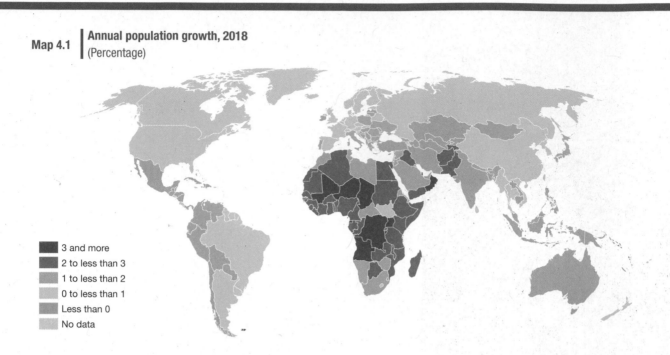

- 3 and more
- 2 to less than 3
- 1 to less than 2
- 0 to less than 1
- Less than 0
- No data

Concepts and definitions

The population estimates and projections reported in this chapter represent the population present in an economy (including residents, migrants and refugees) as of the 1st of July of a given year (United Nations, 2019b, 2019c).

The figures for the years from 2015 to 2050 are based on the medium fertility variant projection. This assumes that the average fertility rate of the world will decline from 2.5 births per woman in the period 2010–2015 to 2.2 in the period 2045–2050. United Nations also produce other projection variants. Their outcome is highly dependent on the path that future fertility will take (United Nations, 2019b).

Urban population is defined as the population living in areas classified as urban according to the criteria used by each country or territory (United Nations, 2019d).

Slowdown of world population growth

The steady slowdown in world population growth, taking place since the late 1980s, continued in 2018. The population grew by 1.1 per cent over the year, or 83 million people, to reach a global total of 7.6 billion. In the coming decades, the slowdown in the rate of population growth is projected to continue. By 2050, it is forecast to fall below 0.5 per cent.

The population of Africa is growing especially fast. In 2018, with a rate of 2.5 per cent, it increased at more than double the pace of the world total. Several central African economies, such as Niger, Uganda, Equatorial Guinea, Angola and the Democratic Republic of the Congo, recorded growth rates well above 3 per cent. Rates higher than world average were also common in Western, Southern and South-Eastern Asia and in Central and Western-Andean South America. Developed economies experienced generally low population growth, 0.3 per cent on average. Several Eastern and Southern European economies, as well as Cuba, Venezuela, Syria, Georgia and Japan, saw their population decline.

Figure 4.1.1 | **Annual growth rate of world population**
(Percentage)

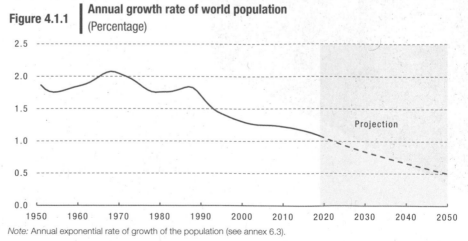

Note: Annual exponential rate of growth of the population (see annex 6.3).

Developing economies drive population growth

Over the last 30 years, the world population has increased by 2.5 billion people. More than 90 per cent of this growth occurred in developing economies, mainly Asia and Oceania. Today, four in five people live in a developing economy. In 1988, this was only the case for three in four.

In the next 30 years, the world is projected to host an additional 2.0 billion. Most of that increase will be accounted for by the developing world. The population of Africa alone will grow by 1.1 billion. One fourth of the world population will live in Africa, as compared to one sixth today.

Figure 4.1.2 | **World population by group of economies** (Billions)

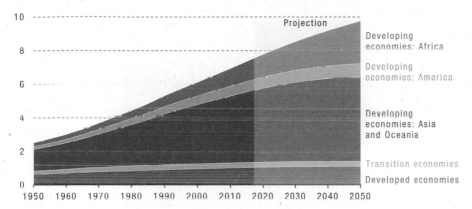

Urbanization continues

All over the world, a growing proportion of the population lives in cities. Ten years ago, 50.6 per cent lived in urban areas. By 2018, the share of urban population increased to 55.3 per cent. It is generally higher in the developed (80 per cent in 2018) than in the developing world (51 per cent), with transition economies in between the two (65 per cent).

Over the last ten years, urbanization has been most pronounced in developing economies, especially in developing Asia and Oceania, which saw the urbanization rate increase from 41.5 in 2008 to 48.5 per cent in 2018. By contrast, further urbanization in the developing economies of America has been relatively modest. But urbanization levels in this region are already comparable to developed economies' levels.

Figure 4.1.3 | **Urban population by group of economies,** (Percentage of total population)

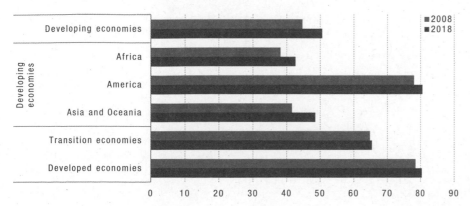

In **2018** the world population **grew by 83 million** people

4 out of 5 live in a **developing** economy

By 2048, an **additional 2 billion** people will live on earth

Proportion of urban population increased from 50.6% to **55.3%** over the last decade

Table 4.1.1 | Total population by group of economies

Group of economies	Population (Millions)			Annual growth rate[a] (Percentage)		
	2013	2018	2050	2013–2018	2018	2018–2050
World	**7 211**	**7 631**	**9 735**	**1.1**	**1.1**	**0.8**
Developing economies	5 865	6 260	8 318	1.3	1.3	0.9
Developing economies: Africa	1 122	1 275	2 488	2.6	2.5	2.1
Developing economies: America	606	638	759	1.0	1.0	0.5
Developing economies: Asia and Oceania	4 137	4 347	5 072	1.0	0.9	0.5
Transition economies	304	310	315	0.4	0.4	0.1
Developed economies	1 042	1 061	1 102	0.4	0.3	0.1
Selected groups						
Developing economies excluding China	4 473	4 832	6 916	1.5	1.5	1.1
Developing economies excluding LDCs	4 967	5 250	6 441	1.1	1.1	0.6
LDCs	898	1 010	1 877	2.3	2.3	1.9
LLDCs	452	509	926	2.4	2.4	1.9
SIDS (UNCTAD)	12	13	16	1.1	1.1	0.7
HIPCs (IMF)	626	720	1 482	2.8	2.8	2.3
BRICS	3 072	3 193	3 482	0.8	0.7	0.3
G20	4 656	4 832	5 277	0.7	0.7	0.3

[a] Annual exponential rate of growth (see annex 6.3).

Table 4.1.2 | Urban population by group of economies

Group of economies	Urban population (Millions)			Share in total population (Percentage)		
	2013	2018	2050	2013	2018	2050
World	**3 823**	**4 220**	**6 656**	**53.0**	**55.3**	**68.4**
Developing economies	2 798	3 165	5 458	47.7	50.6	65.6
Developing economies: Africa	452	543	1 470	40.3	42.6	59.1
Developing economies: America	481	514	665	79.3	80.5	87.7
Developing economies: Asia and Oceania	1 865	2 108	3 323	45.1	48.5	65.5
Transition economies	198	203	234	65.1	65.3	74.1
Developed economies	828	852	965	79.4	80.3	87.6
Selected groups						
Developing economies excluding China	2 060	2 320	4 336	46.1	48.0	62.7
Developing economies excluding LDCs	2 520	2 826	4 473	50.7	53.8	69.4
LDCs	278	339	985	31.0	33.6	52.5
LLDCs	133	157	422	29.5	30.8	45.5
SIDS (UNCTAD)	5	6	9	45.1	45.8	55.7
HIPCs (IMF)	210	258	793	33.6	35.9	53.5
BRICS	1 460	1 633	2 374	47.5	51.1	68.2
G20	2 650	2 884	3 901	56.9	59.7	73.9

Table 4.1.3 | Most populated economies

Economy	Total			Urban		
	Population	Annual growth rate[a]		Share in total population	Annual growth rate[a]	
	(Millions)	(Percentage)		(Percentage)	(Percentage)	
	2018	2013–2018	2018–2050	2018	2013–2018	2018–2050
China	1 428	0.5	-0.1	59.2	2.7	0.9
India	1 353	1.1	0.6	34.0	2.3	2.0
United States of America	330	0.6	0.5	82.4	0.9	0.7
Indonesia	268	1.2	0.7	55.3	2.5	1.5
Pakistan	212	2.1	1.5	36.7	2.7	2.6
Brazil	209	0.8	0.3	86.6	1.1	0.5
Nigeria	196	2.6	2.2	50.3	4.4	3.3
Bangladesh	161	1.1	0.6	36.6	3.3	2.0
Russian Federation	146	0.2	-0.2	74.4	0.3	0.1
Japan	127	-0.2	-0.6	91.6	-0.1	-0.5
Mexico	126	1.2	0.6	80.2	1.6	0.9
Ethiopia	109	2.7	2.0	20.8	4.9	3.9
Philippines	107	1.5	0.9	46.9	1.9	1.8
Egypt	98	2.1	1.5	42.7	2.1	2.3
Viet Nam	96	1.0	0.4	35.9	3.1	1.9
Dem. Rep. of the Congo	84	3.3	2.6	44.5	4.6	3.7
Germany	83	0.5	-0.1	77.3	0.5	0.2
Turkey	82	1.6	0.5	75.1	2.3	0.9
Iran (Islamic Republic of)	82	1.3	0.7	74.9	2.1	1.2
Thailand	69	0.4	-0.2	49.9	1.9	0.9

[a] Annual exponential rate of growth (see annex 6.3).

4.2 Age structure

Map 4.2 | **Dependency ratio, 2018**
(Percentage)

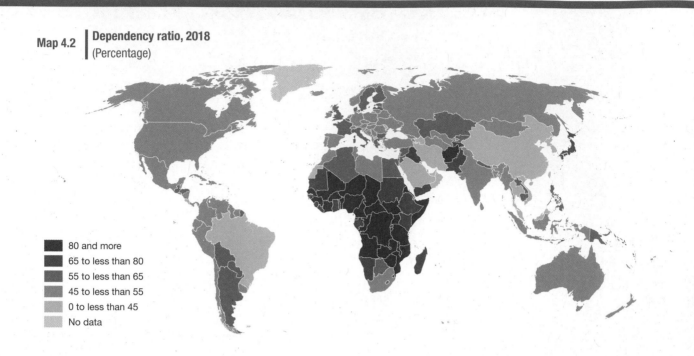

- 80 and more
- 65 to less than 80
- 55 to less than 65
- 45 to less than 55
- 0 to less than 45
- No data

Concepts and definitions

In this section, the term "persons of working age" refers to persons aged from 15 to 64 years. The term "children" refers to persons under the age of 15. The term "older persons" refers to persons aged 65 years or more.

The dependency ratio is defined as the number of children and older persons per hundred persons of working age. It can be expressed as the sum of the child dependency ratio and the old-age dependency ratio.

The child dependency ratio is defined as the number of children per hundred persons of working age.

The old-age dependency ratio is defined as the number of older persons per hundred persons of working age.

Regional distribution of dependency ratios and trends over time

Globally, in 2018, for every 100 persons of working age there were 53 persons who were younger or older. This figure, the dependency ratio, varies considerably across regions. In most economies of Western, Middle and Eastern Africa it is higher than 65 per cent, whereas in Western, Eastern and South-Eastern Asia, it is often lower than 45 per cent. Notable exceptions include Japan (67 per cent) and Israel (66 per cent), as well as Yemen (74 per cent), Timor-Leste (73 per cent), Iraq (72 per cent) and economies around the Hindu Kush.

Of the global ratio of 53 per cent, 14 persons per 100 were younger than the working age and 39 were older. The proportion of people under 15 in the population has steadily declined since 1966, from 38 per cent to 26 per cent in 2018, while the proportion of the older than 64 has risen from 5 to 9 per cent. The net effect has been a decline of the dependency ratio from 76 to 53 per cent. The aging of the world population is projected to continue in the next 30 years.

Figure 4.2.1 | **World population by age group**
(Percentage)

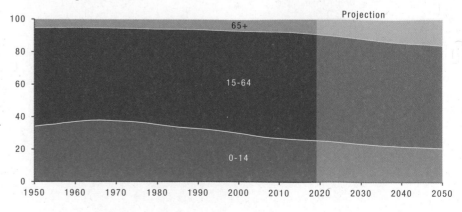

Non-pyramid shape of developed economies' population pyramid

Looking at population pyramids, we find that in developing economies, older age classes are successively smaller than younger. In developed economies, this pattern is reversed, from age 50 years or less, so that the proportions of older age groups are larger and those of younger age groups smaller than in developing economies.

In both the developing and developed world, women are the majority for older age groups, whereas the majority of children are boys. In 2018, 49.6 per cent of the world population were female.

$\frac{2}{3}$ of the **population** are of **working age**

Figure 4.2.2 | **Population pyramids, 2018**

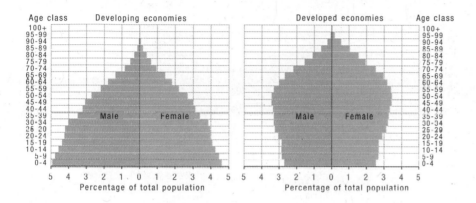

Proportion of young people **fell** from 38 **to 26%** over the last 50 years

Less child dependency, more old-age dependency

Over the next 30 years, the total dependency ratio is projected to rise in most regions. Child dependency ratios will decrease, but it is forecast that this effect will be compensated by rising old-age dependency. Africa is the exception, featuring both decreasing child and overall dependency ratios (child: from 73 per cent in 2018 to 52 per cent in 2050, overall: from 79 to 61 per cent). In general, child dependency ratios are projected to fall fastest where they are currently highest.

Contrary to child dependency, old-age dependency is forecast to increase most for the groups of economies where it is already comparatively high, especially in developed economies, where an increase from 30 to 47 per cent is expected by 2050.

In developed economies, people in their **50s** form the **largest age cohort**

Figure 4.2.3 | **Dependency ratio by age structure** (Percentage)

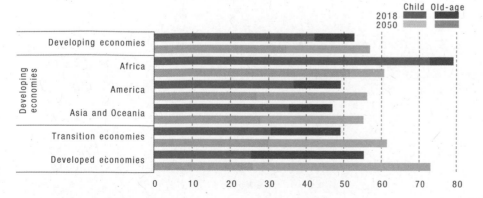

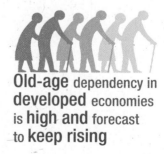

Old-age dependency in **developed** economies is **high and** forecast to **keep rising**

Note: The total dependency ratio is the sum of the child and old-age dependency ratios.

Table 4.2.1 | Age structure by group of economies

Group of economies	Year	Population (Millions)			Dependency ratio (Percentage)		
		0-14	15-64	65+	Child (0-14)	Old-age (65+)	Total
World	1950	870	1 538	129	56.5	8.4	64.9
	2018	1 965	4 988	678	39.4	13.6	53.0
	2050	2 056	6 131	1 549	33.5	25.3	58.8
Developing economies	1950	636	991	64	64.2	6.5	70.7
	2018	1 728	4 097	435	42.2	10.6	52.8
	2050	1 833	5 299	1 185	34.6	22.4	57.0
Developing economies: Africa	1950	94	126	7	74.6	5.9	80.5
	2018	520	711	44	73.1	6.2	79.2
	2050	797	1 548	143	51.5	9.2	60.7
Developing economies: America	1950	67	93	6	72.2	6.2	78.4
	2018	157	428	53	36.7	12.5	49.2
	2050	130	485	144	26.7	29.6	56.3
Developing economies: Asia and Oceania	1950	475	772	51	61.5	6.6	68.1
	2018	1 051	2 958	338	35.5	11.4	47.0
	2050	906	3 266	899	27.8	27.5	55.3
Transition economies	1950	59	128	12	45.7	9.5	55.2
	2018	64	208	39	30.6	18.6	49.2
	2050	58	195	62	29.9	31.6	61.5
Developed economies	1950	175	419	53	41.7	12.5	54.2
	2018	174	683	204	25.5	29.9	55.4
	2050	164	636	302	25.8	47.5	73.3
Selected groups							
Developing economies excluding China	1950	448	650	39	68.9	6.1	74.9
	2018	1 473	3 080	279	47.8	9.1	56.9
	2050	1 635	4 461	819	36.7	18.4	55.0
Developing economies excluding LDCs	1950	556	883	58	62.9	6.5	69.5
	2018	1 330	3 520	399	37.8	11.3	49.1
	2050	1 262	4 113	1 065	30.7	25.9	56.6
LDCs	1950	80	108	6	74.4	5.9	80.3
	2018	398	576	36	69.1	6.2	75.4
	2050	571	1 186	120	48.1	10.1	58.2
LLDCs	1950	32	42	2	76.2	5.4	81.5
	2018	201	289	19	69.4	6.5	75.9
	2050	274	593	60	46.2	10.1	56.3
SIDS (UNCTAD)	1950	2	2	0	69.8	6.9	76.7
	2018	3	8	1	42.1	11.2	53.2
	2050	3	10	2	34.3	22.0	56.3
HIPCs (IMF)	1950	52	67	4	77.3	5.9	83.2
	2018	309	389	22	79.4	5.5	84.9
	2050	484	925	73	52.3	7.9	60.2
BRICS	1950	357	602	39	59.3	6.4	65.7
	2018	709	2 202	283	32.2	12.8	45.0
	2050	574	2 226	682	25.8	30.6	56.4
G20	1950	592	1 104	96	53.6	8.7	62.3
	2018	1 028	3 276	528	31.4	16.1	47.5
	2050	862	3 305	1 110	26.1	33.6	59.7

Table 4.2.2 | Age structure by group of economies, 2018

Group of economies	Population (Millions)	Percentage of total						
		All age classes	0-14	15-24	25-39	40-64	65-74	75+
World	**7 631**	**100.0**	**25.8**	**15.8**	**22.5**	**27.1**	**5.5**	**3.4**
Developing economies	6 260	100.0	27.6	16.7	22.9	25.9	4.6	2.3
Developing economies: Africa	1 275	100.0	40.8	19.3	20.5	16.1	2.4	1.0
Developing economies: America	638	100.0	24.6	16.9	23.4	26.7	5.1	3.3
Developing economies: Asia and Oceania	4 347	100.0	24.2	15.9	23.6	28.6	5.2	2.6
Transition economies	310	100.0	20.5	11.5	24.0	31.6	7.2	5.3
Developed economies	1 061	100.0	16.4	11.5	19.5	33.3	10.4	8.9
Selected groups								
Developing economies excluding China	4 832	100.0	30.5	18.0	22.9	22.8	3.8	2.0
LDCs	1 010	100.0	39.4	20.0	20.6	16.4	2.4	1.1
LLDCs	509	100.0	39.4	19.8	20.6	16.4	2.5	1.2
SIDS (UNCTAD)	13	100.0	27.4	17.3	23.0	25.0	4.6	2.7
Selected economies								
China	1 428	100.0	17.9	12.1	23.0	36.0	7.4	3.5
India	1 353	100.0	27.1	18.2	24.0	24.5	4.2	2.0
Brazil	209	100.0	21.3	16.2	24.5	29.0	5.6	3.4
Nigeria	190	100.0	40.0	19.1	19.0	15.0	2.1	0.7
Russian Federation	146	100.0	17.9	9.5	23.9	34.0	8.4	6.3
Japan	127	100.0	12.7	9.3	16.8	33.6	14.0	13.6

Table 4.2.3 | Female population by age class, 2018

Group of economies	Population (Millions)	Percentage female						
		All age classes	0-14	15-24	25-39	40-64	65-74	75+
World	**3 784**	**49.6**	**48.4**	**48.4**	**49.0**	**50.1**	**52.9**	**58.9**
Developing economies	3 081	49.2	48.3	48.3	48.9	49.8	52.2	56.9
Developing economies: Africa	638	50.0	49.3	49.6	50.2	51.2	54.1	58.2
Developing economies: America	324	50.8	49.0	49.4	50.4	52.1	54.2	59.0
Developing economies: Asia and Oceania	2 119	48.7	47.7	47.7	48.4	49.3	51.6	56.4
Transition economies	163	52.6	48.5	48.8	49.8	53.7	61.1	70.8
Developed economies	540	50.9	48.7	48.8	49.4	50.4	53.0	59.9
Selected groups								
Developing economies excluding China	2 385	49.4	48.6	48.6	49.1	50.1	52.8	57.0
LDCs	508	50.3	49.4	49.7	50.8	51.4	53.9	56.5
LLDCs	257	50.4	49.3	49.7	51.0	52.0	55.5	59.4
SIDS (UNCTAD)	6	49.5	49.0	48.5	48.5	50.5	52.7	56.8
Selected economies								
China	695	48.7	46.5	46.8	48.4	49.3	51.2	56.7
India	650	48.0	47.5	47.1	47.6	48.8	50.9	54.0
Brazil	106	50.8	48.9	49.3	50.1	51.9	54.9	60.3
Nigeria	97	49.3	48.9	49.2	49.3	50.3	52.4	53.3
Russian Federation	78	53.7	48.7	48.9	50.0	54.4	62.6	73.3
Japan	65	51.2	48.7	48.7	48.9	49.6	52.2	60.9

Maritime
transport

KEY FIGURES 2018

Seaborne trade
volume
11.0 billion tons

World commercial
fleet capacity
(as of 31 December)
2.0 billion dwt

Growth in
commercial fleet
capacity
+2.7%

Global container
port traffic
793 million TEUs

5.1 World seaborne trade

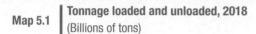

Map 5.1 | **Tonnage loaded and unloaded, 2018**
(Billions of tons)

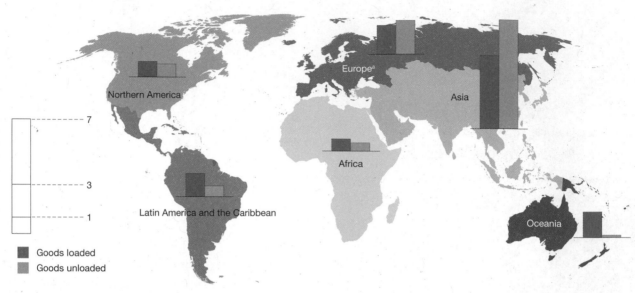

Northern America

Europe[a]

Asia

Africa

Latin America and the Caribbean

Oceania

7

3

1

■ Goods loaded
■ Goods unloaded

[a] Including the Russian Federation and the French overseas departments.

Concepts and definitions

The figures on seaborne trade in this section measure the volumes, in tons, of goods loaded and unloaded in the world's seaports for international shipment. Cabotage and transshipments are not included.

Goods loaded for international shipment are assumed to be exports, while goods unloaded from ships are assumed to be imports. The seaborne trade balance measures the difference between the volumes of loaded and unloaded goods.

Dry cargo refers to cargo that is usually not carried in tankers, such as dry bulks (e.g. coal, ores, grains), pallets, bags, crates, and containers. Other tanker trade refers to refined petroleum products, gas and chemicals.

The data presented in this section have been compiled from various sources, including country reports as well as port industry and other specialist websites.

Trends and geography of world seaborne trade

International seaborne trade lost momentum in 2018, with volumes only increasing at a modest 2.7 per cent, after a surge of 4.1 per cent in 2017. Since 2013, growth in seaborne trade has been relatively sluggish, as compared to the aftermath of the 2009 financial crisis, when annual growth rates ranged between 4.4 and 7 per cent. Nevertheless, in 2018, world seaborne trade volumes rose to a new all-time high of 11 billion tons.

Asia was by far the largest trading region. In 2018, 4.5 billion tons of goods were loaded, and 6.7 billion tons unloaded in Asian seaports. The other continents registered less than half of these amounts.

Of the 11 billion tons shipped internationally in 2018, 7.8 billion tons were classified as dry cargo. Crude oil, the most transported cargo in the 1970s, has lost market share over the last four decades, and by 2018 it accounted for less than one fifth of the goods delivered by sea.

Figure 5.1.1 | **Goods loaded worldwide**
(Billions of tons)

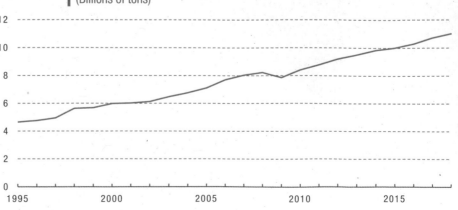

Contribution of developing economies

In 2018, developing economies still accounted for the largest share of global seaborne trade, both in terms of exports (goods loaded) and imports (goods unloaded). They loaded 59 per cent and unloaded 64 per cent of the world total. With a volume of 4.2 billion tons loaded and 5.9 billion tons unloaded, Asian and Oceanian developing economies together accounted for most of that share.

The contribution of developing economies to world maritime exports has declined slightly over time, while their share of imports has risen.

Figure 5.1.2 | **Seaborne trade of developing economies** (Percentage of corresponding world tonnage)

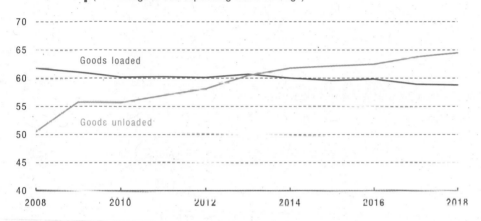

Developments in seaborne trade balances

The declining contribution of seaborne trade exports and increasing contribution of seaborne trade imports has led to a steady reduction of the developing economies' trade balance. As a result, in 2014 they switched from net exporters into net importers. In absolute terms, their balance changed from a surplus of 896 million tons in 2008 into a deficit of 623 million tons in 2018.

Over the same time period, transition economies recorded an increase in their surplus from 343 million tons to 627 million tons. For developed economies, the deficit of 1.3 billion tons recorded in 2008 has fallen. In 2018, they loaded and unloaded an equal volume of goods at their seaports.[1]

[1] For further analyses on that topic, see UNCTAD (2019c).

Figure 5.1.3 | **Seaborne trade balance** (Millions of tons)

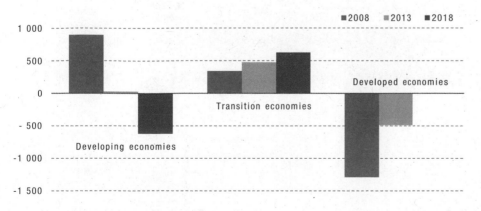

International **seaborne trade** slows: only **+2.7%** in 2018

61% of all goods **unloaded** in **Asian** seaports

Developing economies' **share** of **seaborne** trade **imports** rose to **64% in 2018**

The maritime trade **balance** of **developed** economies **is falling**

Table 5.1.1 | Total seaborne trade by group of economies

Group of economies	Loaded			Unloaded			Balance	
	Volume		Annual growth rate	Volume		Annual growth rate	Volume	
	(Millions of tons)		(Percentage)	(Millions of tons)		(Percentage)	(Millions of tons)	
	2013	2018	2018	2013	2018	2018	2013	2018
World[a]	**9 513**	**11 005**	**2.7**	**9 501**	**11 002**	**2.8**	**12**	**3**
Developing economies	5 774	6 470	2.5	5 745	7 093	3.9	28	-623
Developing economies: Africa	815	767	3.5	433	516	3.9	383	251
Developing economies: America	1 264	1 404	2.3	569	653	5.7	694	751
Developing economies: Asia and Oceania	3 695	4 299	2.4	4 743	5 924	3.7	-1 049	-1 625
Transition economies	551	713	2.7	77	86	6.2	475	627
Developed economies	3 188	3 822	3.0	3 679	3 823	0.7	-491	-1

[a] Annual totals of goods loaded and unloaded are not necessarily the same, given that goods loaded in one calendar year may reach their port of destination in the next calendar year.

Table 5.1.2 | Seaborne trade by cargo type and group of economies

Crude oil

Group of economies	Loaded			Unloaded			Balance	
	Volume		Annual growth rate	Volume		Annual growth rate	Volume	
	(Millions of tons)		(Percentage)	(Millions of tons)		(Percentage)	(Millions of tons)	
	2013	2018	2018	2013	2018	2018	2013	2018
World[a]	**1 738**	**1 886**	**0.6**	**1 882**	**2 048**	**0.7**	**-144**	**-162**
Developing economies	1 478	1 525	0.6	874	1 102	4.5	604	423
Developing economies: Africa	328	289	-0.7	37	42	4.8	291	247
Developing economies: America	240	219	-2.6	69	52	9.0	171	167
Developing economies: Asia and Oceania	911	1 016	1.8	768	1 007	4.3	143	9
Transition economies	145	204	-1.5	1	0	0.0	144	203
Developed economies	114	158	3.3	1 007	947	-3.3	-892	-789

[a] Annual totals of goods loaded and unloaded are not necessarily the same, given that goods loaded in one calendar year may reach their port of destination in the next calendar year.

Other tanker trade

Group of economies	Loaded			Unloaded			Balance	
	Volume		Annual growth rate	Volume		Annual growth rate	Volume	
	(Millions of tons)		(Percentage)	(Millions of tons)		(Percentage)	(Millions of tons)	
	2013	2018	2018	2013	2018	2018	2013	2018
World[a]	**1 091**	**1 308**	**2.9**	**1 096**	**1 322**	**2.5**	**-6**	**-14**
Developing economies	588	757	2.5	529	821	3.9	59	-64
Developing economies: Africa	82	74	4.8	65	94	0.1	17	-20
Developing economies: America	70	78	8.9	89	149	5.3	-20	-71
Developing economies: Asia and Oceania	436	605	1.5	375	578	4.2	61	27
Transition economies	32	40	-4.8	11	5	4.3	21	35
Developed economies	471	511	4.1	557	496	0.2	-86	15

[a] Annual totals of goods loaded and unloaded are not necessarily the same, given that goods loaded in one calendar year may reach their port of destination in the next calendar year.

Dry cargo

Group of economies	Loaded			Unloaded			Balance	
	Volume		Annual growth rate	Volume		Annual growth rate	Volume	
	(Millions of tons)		(Percentage)	(Millions of tons)		(Percentage)	(Millions of tons)	
	2013	2018	2018	2013	2018	2018	2013	2018
World[a]	**6 685**	**7 811**	**3.2**	**6 523**	**7 632**	**3.4**	**162**	**179**
Developing economies	3 707	4 188	3.2	4 342	5 170	3.8	-635	-982
Developing economies: Africa	405	404	6.6	331	380	4.8	75	24
Developing economies: America	954	1 106	2.9	411	452	5.5	543	654
Developing economies: Asia and Oceania	2 348	2 678	2.8	3 601	4 338	3.5	-1 253	-1 660
Transition economies	374	470	5.4	65	81	6.4	309	389
Developed economies	2 603	3 153	2.9	2 116	2 381	2.6	487	772

[a] Annual totals of goods loaded and unloaded are not necessarily the same, given that goods loaded in one calendar year may reach their port of destination in the next calendar year.

Table 5.1.3 | **Development of goods loaded worldwide by type of cargo**
(Millions of tons)

Year	Total goods	Crude oil	Other tanker trade	Dry cargo
1973	3 274	1 514	353	1 407
1978	3 550	1 604	296	1 650
1983	3 231	1 069	392	1 770
1988	3 735	1 160	456	2 119
1993	4 330	1 443	502	2 386
1998	5 631	1 548	534	3 549
2003	6 480	1 690	533	4 257
2008	8 231	1 785	957	5 489
2013	9 513	1 738	1 001	6 685
2018	11 005	1 886	1 308	7 811

5.2 Merchant fleet

Map 5.2 | **Building, ownership, registration and scrapping of ships, 2018**
(Percentage of world total)

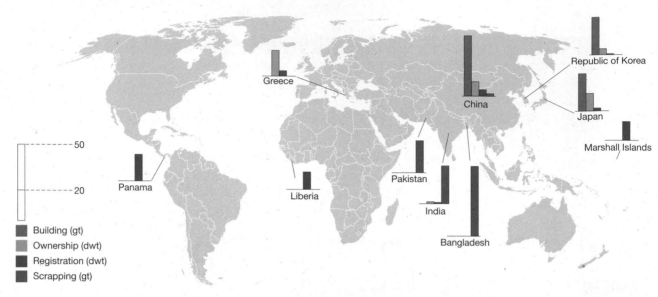

Sources: UNCTADstat (UNCTAD, 2019a), Clarksons Research.
Note: Top three countries in each segment are shown; building and scrapping are estimated deliveries and demolitions during 2018; registration and ownership are end-of-year figures.

Concepts and definitions

The unit dead-weight tons (dwt) is used to indicate the cargo carrying capacity of a ship, while gross tons (gt) reflect its size. The latter is relevant to measure shipbuilding and scrapping activity, while the former is used to capture the capacity to transport cargo.

Statistics on fleet registration (the flag of a ship), shipbuilding and scrapping is for all commercial ships of 100 gt and more. The market shares for ownership only cover larger ships of 1000 gt and above, as the true ownership is not always known for smaller vessels.

World fleet development and composition

In January 2019, the world fleet reached a carrying capacity of 1.98 billion dwt, 52 million dwt more than the previous year. Over recent years, tonnage has increased considerably in all segments except general cargo carriers. Bulk carriers recorded an especially rapid increase. Between 2009 and 2019, their share of total carrying capacity rose from 35 to 43 per cent, whereas the shares of oil tankers and general cargo shrank from 35 to 29 per cent and from 9 to 4 per cent, respectively.

Shipbuilding and scrapping

In 2018, 90 per cent of global shipbuilding, in terms of tonnage, was located in China, the Republic of Korea and Japan. Bangladesh, India and Pakistan accounted for 92 per cent of ship scrapping.

Figure 5.2.1 | **World fleet by principal vessel type**
(Millions of dead-weight tons)

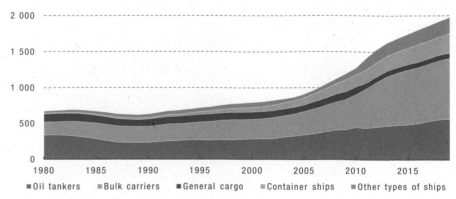

Sources: UNCTADstat (UNCTAD, 2019a); Clarksons Research.
Note: Commercial ships of 100 gt and above; beginning-of-year figures.

Fleet ownership

As of January 2019, the top five ship-owning economies combined accounted for 51 per cent of world fleet tonnage. Greece held a market share of 18 per cent, followed by Japan (11 per cent), China (11 per cent), Singapore (6 per cent), and Hong Kong SAR (5 per cent). Almost half of the world's tonnage was owned by Asian companies. Owners from Europe accounted for 41 per cent and from Northern America for 6 per cent. Companies from Latin America and the Caribbean, Africa and Oceania had shares of one per cent or less.

Figure 5.2.2 | **Fleet market size by region of beneficial ownership, 2019**
(Millions of dead-weight tons)

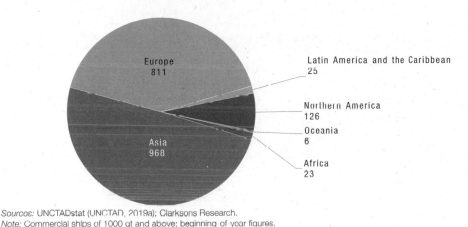

Sources: UNCTADstat (UNCTAD, 2019a); Clarksons Research.
Note: Commercial ships of 1000 gt and above; beginning of year figures.

Major flags of registration

Many commercial ships are registered under a flag that does not match the nationality of the vessel owner. For example, at the begining of 2019, one half of all ships owned by Japanese entities were registered in Panama; one fifth of the ships owned by Greek entities were registered in the Marshall Islands, and another fifth in Liberia.

Panama (333 million dwt), Marshall Islands (246 million dwt) and Liberia (243 million dwt) were the leading flags of registration. Hong Kong SAR and Singapore followed in fourth and fifth place. Among these five, Marshall Islands have recorded the strongest increase in registrations in recent years.

Figure 5.2.3 | **Vessels capacity in top 5 registries**
(Millions of dead-weight tons)

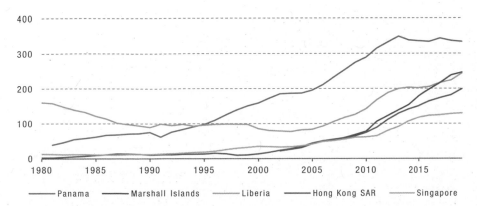

Sources: UNCTADstat (UNCTAD, 2019a); Clarksons Research.
Note: Commercial ships of 100 gt and above; ranked by the values as of 1 January 2019.

World commercial fleet grew by 52 million dwt in 2018

90% of global shipbuilding occured in China, the Republic of Korea and Japan in 2018

Half of the world fleet is owned by Asian companies

Ships with a total capacity of $\frac{1}{3}$ billion dwt registered in Panama

Table 5.2.1 | Merchant fleet registration by group of economies

Group of economies	2014 Tonnage (Millions of dwt)	2014 Tonnage Share in world (Percentage)	2014 Vessels (Thousands)	2014 Vessels Share in world (Percentage)	2019 Tonnage (Millions of dwt)	2019 Tonnage Share in world (Percentage)	2019 Vessels (Thousands)	2019 Vessels Share in world (Percentage)
World	**1 689**	**100.0**	**88**	**100.0**	**1 976**	**100.0**	**96**	**100.0**
Developing economies	1 280	75.8	58	65.5	1 512	76.5	65	67.9
Developing economies: Africa	229	13.5	6	6.9	260	13.1	7	7.4
Developing economies: America	450	26.6	16	18.5	449	22.7	16	16.6
Developing economies: Asia and Oceania	601	35.6	35	40.1	803	40.6	42	43.9
Transition economies	10	0.6	4	4.3	11	0.6	4	4.1
Developed economies	395	23.4	25	28.7	449	22.7	26	26.6
Selected groups								
Developing economies excluding China	1 202	71.2	54	60.9	1 420	71.9	60	62.1
Developing economies excluding LDCs	1 050	62.2	51	58.2	1 255	63.5	59	60.9
LDCs	230	13.6	6	7.3	257	13.0	7	7.0
LLDCs	3	0.2	1	1.2	3	0.1	1	1.1
SIDS (UNCTAD)	254	15.1	8	8.7	345	17.4	9	9.0
HIPCs (IMF)	220	13.0	5	5.9	250	12.7	6	6.1
BRICS	105	6.2	9	10.0	124	6.3	11	11.5
G20	511	30.3	43	49.4	598	30.3	49	50.4

Sources: UNCTADstat (UNCTAD, 2019a); Clarksons Research.
Note: Commercial ships of 100 gt and above; beginning-of-year figures.

Table 5.2.2 | Fleet ownership and registration, main economies, 1 January 2019

Vessels
(Number of vessels)

Economy of ownership (Ranked by number of ships owned)	Flag of registration (Ranked by number of ships registered)							
	Panama	China	Liberia	Marshall Islands	Singapore	China, Hong Kong SAR	Indonesia	World
China	573	3 987	60	53	51	905	7	6 125
Greece	454	0	958	952	32	20	1	4 536
Japan	2 060	0	178	189	128	58	9	3 822
Singapore	257	2	152	122	1 511	131	87	2 727
Germany	32	1	673	137	70	20	0	2 672
Indonesia	17	1	7	0	7	4	2 062	2 145
Norway	54	0	85	126	95	41	4	2 038
United States of America	74	0	95	356	6	49	0	1 978
Russian Federation	35	0	130	1	2	1	0	1 707
Korea, Republic of	455	0	43	265	3	25	5	1 647
World	**6 465**	**4 039**	**3 456**	**3 454**	**2 600**	**2 442**	**2 216**	**51 684**

Sources: UNCTADstat (UNCTAD, 2019a); Clarksons Research.
Note: Commercial ships of 1000 gt and above; beginning-of-year figures.

Tonnage
(Thousands of dead-weight tons)

Economy of ownership (Ranked by tonnage owned)	Flag of registration (Ranked by tonnage registered)							
	Panama	Marshall Islands	Liberia	China, Hong Kong SAR	Singapore	Malta	China	World
Greece	25 642	71 339	76 272	1 191	2 175	65 774	0	349 195
Japan	134 705	11 944	14 686	2 990	7 408	491	0	225 121
China	20 898	2 485	3 365	75 268	4 656	2 687	90 930	206 301
Singapore	9 377	7 455	12 064	6 845	71 287	889	52	121 486
China, Hong Kong SAR	9 458	2 736	6 215	72 311	3 613	307	192	98 128
Germany	865	7 694	36 396	1 316	3 690	7 707	34	96 532
Korea, Republic of	34 917	24 553	1 682	1 219	10	183	0	76 702
Norway	3 105	5 941	4 141	6 185	2 781	1 328	0	61 115
United States of America	1 186	27 091	6 876	3 325	183	377	0	58 382
Bermuda	2 628	17 346	3 757	7 403	1 077	266	0	58 232
World	**332 809**	**245 745**	**243 112**	**198 686**	**129 363**	**110 653**	**91 499**	**1 962 582**

Sources: UNCTADstat (UNCTAD, 2019a); Clarksons Research.
Note: Commercial ships of 1000 gt and above; beginning-of-year figures.

5.3 Maritime transport indicators

Map 5.3 | **Liner shipping connectivity, 2019**

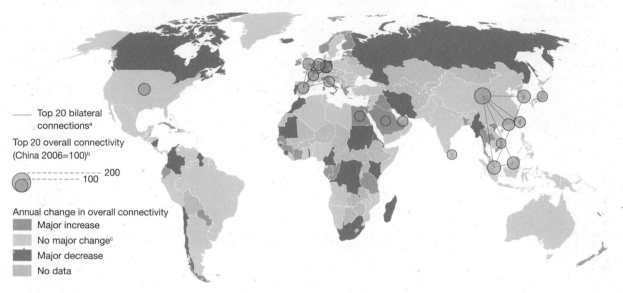

— Top 20 bilateral connections[a]

Top 20 overall connectivity (China 2006=100)[b]

200
100

Annual change in overall connectivity
- Major increase
- No major change[c]
- Major decrease
- No data

[a] As indicated by the LSBCI.
[b] As indicated by the LSCI.
[c] Change of less than 5 per cent compared to the value in the previous year.

Concepts and definitions

The liner shipping connectivity index (LSCI) is an indicator of a country's position within the global liner shipping networks. It is calculated from the number of ships, their container carrying capacity, the number of services and companies, and the size of the largest ship.

The liner shipping bilateral connectivity index (LSBCI) is calculated from five components, including the number of transshipments required to trade and the number of options available to use only one transshipment.

Port container traffic is measured in twenty-foot equivalent units (TEUs). One TEU represents the volume of a standard 20 feet long intermodal container used for loading, unloading, repositioning and transshipment.

The number of port calls and the time spent in ports are derived from the fusion of automatic identification system data with port mapping intelligence, covering ships of 1000 gt and above.

Liner shipping connectivity throughout the world

In 2019, the economy best connected to the global liner shipping network, as measured by the LSCI, was China. Singapore, the Republic of Korea, Malaysia and the United States of America followed next in the rankings. Sub-regional leaders comprised: Belgium, Netherlands and the United Kingdom in Europe; Panama, Mexico and Colombia in Latin America and the Caribbean; Egypt, Morocco and South Africa in Africa; and Sri Lanka in South Asia. The Russian Federation and Ukraine were the best-connected transition economies. All top-20 bilateral connections were intra-regional, namely within Europe and within Eastern and South-Eastern Asia.

Over the last ten years, China and the Republic of Korea have developed particularly strong improvements in connectivity, allowing China to maintain their lead and the Republic of Korea to approach second place.

Figure 5.3.1 | **Liner shipping connectivity index, top five economies** (China 2006 = 100)

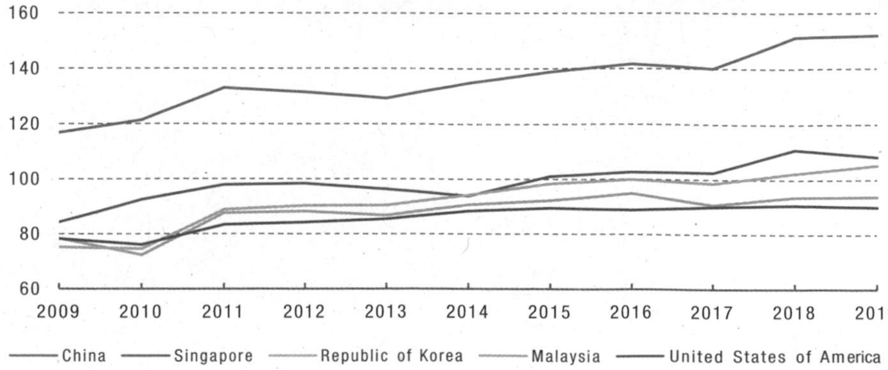

— China — Singapore — Republic of Korea — Malaysia — United States of America

Port container traffic

In 2018, 793 million TEUs of containers were handled in ports worldwide. World container port throughput grew by 4.7 per cent between 2017 and 2018. Thus some momentum was lost – in tandem with world seaborne trade (see section 5.1) – after a year of significant growth (+6.7 per cent) from 2016 to 2017.

Figure 5.3.2 | **World container port throughput**
(Millions of twenty-foot equivalent units)

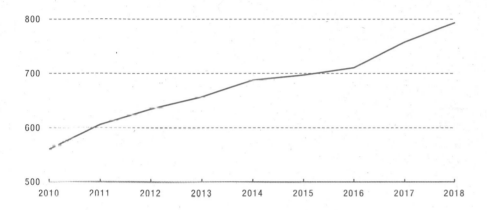

Regional activity

Asia's role as a main port loading and unloading region (see section 5.1) and its high liner shipping connectivity is reflected in the region's high contribution to containerized port throughput. In 2018, ports in developing economies in Asia and Oceania handled 485 million TEUs of containers, accounting for 61 per cent of world port container traffic. The shares of developing economies in America (7 per cent) and Africa (4 per cent) were much smaller. Developed economies accounted for about 25 per cent and transition economies for less than one per cent.

The economy that recorded most port calls of ships, including ferries, roll-on roll-off and passenger ships, in 2018, was Norway.[1]

[1] For further analyses on that topic, see UNCTAD (2019c).

Figure 5.3.3 | **Containerized port traffic by group of economies, 2018**
(Millions of twenty-foot equivalent units)

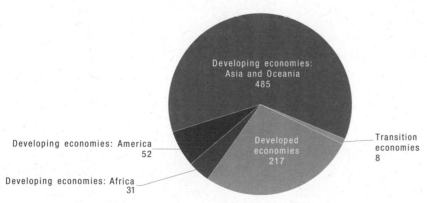

China, Singapore and the **Republic of Korea** are **best integrated** into the global liner **shipping networks**

Bilateral **connectivity** is **highest within continents**, rather than between

Growth in container port throughput moderated in 2018: +4.7%

Developing economies in **Asia and Oceania** handled 61% of world port **container traffic**

Table 5.3.1 | **Liner shipping connectivity index of most connected economies, by region**
(China 2006 = 100)

	Economy (Ranked by 2019 value)	2009	2014	2018	2019
Northern America and Europe	1. United States of America	78	88	91	90
	2. Belgium	85	79	88	88
	3. Netherlands	81	82	89	88
	4. United Kingdom	77	77	89	85
	5. Spain	76	83	86	84
Latin America and the Caribbean	1. Panama	32	42	50	49
	2. Mexico	35	39	46	45
	3. Colombia	29	39	48	45
	4. Peru	21	32	39	39
	5. Dominican Republic	25	28	40	39
Africa	1. Egypt	46	57	62	67
	2. Morocco	37	58	65	58
	3. South Africa	33	38	38	35
	4. Djibouti	22	21	35	31
	5. Togo	14	19	32	29
Asia	1. China	117	135	151	152
	2. Singapore	84	94	111	108
	3. Korea, Republic of	75	94	102	105
	4. Malaysia	78	91	94	94
	5. China, Hong Kong SAR	89	93	94	89
Oceania	1. Australia	31	34	34	34
	2. New Zealand	23	24	23	32
	3. Papua New Guinea	11	12	13	13
	4. Fiji	14	14	13	11
	5. New Caledonia	14	14	12	11

Note: Beginning of year figures.

5

Table 5.3.2 | **Time at port, by market segment, in the top 20 economies by port call, 2018**

Economy	Number of arrivals	Median time at port (days)						
		All market segments	Wet bulk	Container ship	Dry breakbulk	Dry bulk	LPG carriers	LNG carriers
1 Norway	524 469	0.4	0.6	0.3	0.3	0.9	0.8	0.3
2 United States of America[a]	280 332	1.4	1.6	1.0	1.8	1.8	2.0	1.3
3 Japan	265 518	0.4	0.3	0.4	1.1	0.9	0.3	1.0
4 China	240 385	1.0	1.1	0.6	1.2	2.0	1.0	1.2
5 Italy	229 930	1.3	1.3	0.8	1.9	3.6	1.4	..
6 United Kingdom[b]	193 462	1.1	1.1	0.7	1.5	2.7	1.1	1.4
7 Turkey	184 169	1.2	1.1	0.6	1.5	4.0	1.4	1.3
8 Greece	155 072	0.7	0.5	1.0	1.1	0.4	0.9	1.0
9 Indonesia	150 429	1.3	1.3	1.1	1.3	3.6	1.1	1.4
10 Spain	139 717	0.9	0.8	0.7	1.1	2.3	1.0	1.1
11 Netherlands	123 726	0.6	0.5	0.8	0.4	0.8	0.9	1.3
12 Denmark	113 642	0.7	0.7	0.5	0.8	0.9	1.1	..
13 Germany	100 013	0.6	0.4	0.8	0.5	2.5	0.8	..
14 Canada	86 533	0.7	1.1	1.5	0.3	0.3	..	..
15 Russian Federation	81 187	1.3	1.0	1.4	1.6	2.5	1.3	1.1
16 Sweden	79 238	0.8	0.7	0.6	1.0	0.5	0.8	0.6
17 Korea, Republic of	71 602	0.8	0.8	0.6	1.3	2.3	0.7	1.0
18 France[c]	68 739	1.1	1.1	0.8	1.5	3.1	1.1	1.2
19 Croatia	68 378	1.2	1.0	0.6	2.6	1.8	..	..
20 Australia	62 029	1.5	1.3	1.2	1.8	1.7	0.9	1.2

[a] Excluding Puerto Rico and United States Virgin Islands.
[b] United Kingdom of Great Britain and Northern Ireland excluding Channel Islands and Isle of Man.
[c] Excluding French Guiana, Guadeloupe, Martinique, Mayotte, Monaco and Reunion.
Note: Total arrivals include arrivals of ferries, roll-on roll-off and passenger ships, for which the time in port is not computed.

Table 5.3.3 | **Liner shipping bilateral connectivity indices of the world's seven most connected economies**

Economy (Ranked by LSCI 2019)	Year	LSCI (China 2006=100)	Liner shipping bilateral connectivity index vis-à-vis ...						
			China	Singapore	Korea, Rep. of	Malaysia	United States of America	China, Hong Kong SAR	Belgium
China	2014	135	–	0.747	0.816	0.777	0.692	0.811	0.690
	2019	152	–	0.786	0.853	0.755	0.679	0.752	0.716
Singapore	2014	94		–	0.668	0.773	0.608	0.686	0.645
	2019	108		–	0.748	0.791	0.630	0.669	0.698
Korea, Republic of	2014	94			–	0.698	0.644	0.727	0.619
	2019	105			–	0.709	0.655	0.702	0.659
Malaysia	2014	91				–	0.600	0.732	0.654
	2019	94				–	0.585	0.646	0.651
United States of America	2014	88					–	0.642	0.636
	2019	90					–	0.594	0.680
China, Hong Kong SAR	2014	93						–	0.644
	2019	89						–	0.627
Belgium	2014	79							–
	2019	88							–

Annexes

6.1 Key indicators by economy, 2018

Economy	Merchandise trade			Trade in services		GDP	
	Exports	Imports	Terms of trade	Exports	Imports	Per capita (nominal)	Growth (real)[a]
	(Millions of US$)	(Millions of US$)	(2015=100)	(Millions of US$)	(Millions of US$)	(US$)	(Percentage)
World	**19 453 362**	**19 793 724**	**101**	**5 845 070**	**5 603 620**	**11 181**	**3.0**
Developing economies	8 657 105	8 321 958	100	1 738 140	2 118 210	5 405	4.2
Developing economies: Africa	483 940	576 221	113	118 040	177 980	1 851	2.9
Algeria	41 168	46 197	115	(e) 3 131	(e) 10 915	4 267	1.9
Angola	40 758	15 798	128	631	10 087	3 637	-0.9
Benin	2 451	4 068	110	(e) 574	(e) 741	901	6.1
Botswana	6 587	6 287	93	(e) 1 046	(e) 932	8 413	4.4
Burkina Faso	3 253	4 451	107	(e) 526	(e) 1 511	720	6.4
Burundi	180	793	101	-	-	286	-0.5
Cabo Verde	76	816	100	698	384	3 612	4.5
Cameroon	3 801	6 128	108	-	-	1 524	3.9
Central African Republic	(e) 152	(e) 430	100	-	-	480	4.3
Chad	(e) 2 000	(e) 2 170	126	-	-	767	3.4
Comoros	42	284	56	-	-	1 444	3.7
Congo	(e) 10 034	(e) 3 470	124	-	-	2 693	1.2
Côte d'Ivoire	12 322	(e) 10 968	90	(e) 1 025	(e) 3 238	1 712	7.2
Dem. Rep. of the Congo	(e) 8 800	(e) 5 200	118	-	-	477	3.9
Djibouti	(e) 168	(e) 804	101	(e) 451	(e) 224	2 075	6.8
Egypt	27 624	72 000	106	(e) 23 567	(e) 18 697	2 537	5.3
Equatorial Guinea	(e) 6 500	(e) 2 210	124	-	-	10 533	-6.8
Eritrea	(e) 683	(e) 1 170	111	-	-	1 943	4.0
Eswatini	1 827	1 878	101	(e) 96	(e) 271	4 158	1.3
Ethiopia	(e) 2 831	(e) 15 500	94	(e) 4 909	(e) 6 770	731	7.3
French Southern Territories	..	..	..	..	..	..	..
Gabon	(e) 7 082	(e) 3 061	126	-	-	7 938	1.9
Gambia	(e) 102	(e) 551	100	-	-	704	5.3
Ghana	14 868	13 089	111	(e) 7 572	(e) 10 080	2 209	6.5
Guinea	3 978	3 386	107	(e) 94	(e) 767	967	5.9
Guinea-Bissau	349	330	109	(e) 31	(e) 173	779	3.9
Kenya	6 052	17 378	98	(e) 5 319	(e) 3 691	1 639	5.9
Lesotho	1 175	(e) 2 228	91	32	353	1 359	2.0
Liberia	490	1 100	111	-	-	577	3.0
Lybia	24 814	12 833	118	-	-	5 159	11.0
Madagascar	3 052	4 031	84	-	-	530	5.1
Malawi	1 046	2 795	97	(e) 158	(e) 360	386	2.5
Mali	3 437	4 770	104	(e) 514	(e) 2 429	898	5.4
Mauritania	(e) 1 885	(e) 2 581	111	-	-	1 204	3.2
Mauritius	2 372	5 667	94	3 186	2 184	11 366	3.7
Morocco	28 609	51 038	109	18 541	10 552	3 276	2.8
Mozambique	(e) 5 196	(e) 6 786	113	(e) 673	(e) 4 166	493	3.2

Current account balance	FDI		CPI growth	Population			Fleet size[b]	Economy
	Outflows	Inflows		Total	Share of urban	Old-age dependency ratio		
(Millions of US$)	(Millions of US$)	(Millions of US$)	(Percentage)	(Thousands)	(Percentage)	(Percentage)	(1000 of dwt)	
370 057	**1 014 173**	**1 297 153**	**3.2**	**7 631 091**	**55.3**	**13.6**	**1 976 491**	**World**
167 404	417 554	706 043	5.0	6 259 661	50.6	10.6	1 512 438	Developing economies
-76 764	9 801	45 902	10.9	1 274 779	42.6	6.2	259 661	Developing economies: Africa
(e) -16 419	880	1 506	4.3	42 228	72.6	10.0	658	Algeria
7 403	3	-5 732	20.2	30 810	65.5	4.3	315	Angola
(e) -926	24	208	1.0	11 485	47.3	6.0	0	Benin
345	125	229	3.2	2 254	69.4	6.9	..	Botswana
-	69	480	1.9	10 751	29.4	4.6	..	Burkina Faso
(e) -459	0	1	-2.8	11 175	13.0	4.3	..	Burundi
-104	-20	100	1.3	544	65.7	6.9	39	Cabo Verde
(e) -1 555	-9	702	1.1	25 216	56.4	5.0	440	Cameroon
-187	..	18	3.0	4 666	41.4	5.3	..	Central African Republic
-429	..	662	2.5	15 478	23.1	4.9	..	Chad
-68	..	8	2.0	832	29.0	5.2	1 070	Comoros
2 382	14	4 313	1.2	5 244	66.9	4.8	5	Congo
(e) -1 459	318	913	0.4	25 069	50.8	5.2	10	Côte d'Ivoire
2 160	209	1 494	29.3	84 068	44.5	5.9	26	Dem. Rep. of the Congo
(e) -192	..	265	0.1	959	77.8	6.9	6	Djibouti
-8 293	324	6 798	20.9	98 424	42.7	8.6	1 542	Egypt
-762	..	396	1.1	1 309	72.1	4.1	49	Equatorial Guinea
-	..	61	9.0	3 453	40.1	8.4	14	Eritrea
(e) 462	-11	25	4.8	1 136	23.8	6.9	..	Eswatini
(e) -5 253	..	3 310	13.8	109 224	20.8	6.3	336	Ethiopia
..	..	..	..	..	..	..	3	French Southern Territories
-332	-63	846	4.7	2 119	89.4	6.0	395	Gabon
(e) -185	-6	29	6.5	2 280	61.3	4.9	4	Gambia
(p) -2 072	81	2 989	9.8	29 767	56.1	5.2	37	Ghana
-191	0	483	9.8	12 414	36.1	5.5	0	Guinea
-	1	17	1.4	1 874	43.4	5.1	1	Guinea-Bissau
(c) 4 801	164	1 626	4.7	51 393	27.0	4.0	9	Kenya
-114	..	39	4.0	2 108	28.2	7.9	..	Lesotho
..	84	122	23.6	4 819	51.2	5.8	243 129	Liberia
889	315	..	23.1	6 679	80.1	6.5	1 616	Lybia
80	0	349	7.3	26 262	37.2	5.3	9	Madagascar
(e) -1 288	6	102	12.4	18 143	16.9	4.9	..	Malawi
(e) -1 254	55	366	1.7	19 078	42.4	5.0	..	Mali
(e) -937	4	71	3.1	4 403	53.7	5.5	1	Mauritania
-815	83	372	3.2	1 267	40.8	16.2	123	Mauritius
-6 445	666	3 640	1.9	36 029	62.5	10.7	129	Morocco
-4 362	-19	2 711	3.9	29 496	36.0	5.5	27	Mozambique

Economy	Merchandise trade			Trade in services		GDP	
	Exports	Imports	Terms of trade	Exports	Imports	Per capita (nominal)	Growth (real)[a]
	(Millions of US$)	(Millions of US$)	(2015=100)	(Millions of US$)	(Millions of US$)	(US$)	(Percentage)
Namibia	(e) 5 395	8 329	102	760	659	5 670	-0.1
Niger	1 293	2 218	99	(e) 254	(e) 1 085	411	5.3
Nigeria	60 547	43 007	121	(e) 4 810	(e) 30 836	2 153	1.9
Rwanda	1 126	2 518	112	(e) 1 093	(e) 1 059	773	8.6
Saint Helena	(e) 78	(e) 36	110	..	..	..	..
Sao Tome and Principe	16	148	80	(e) 95	(e) 66	2 132	3.3
Senegal	3 623	8 072	103	(e) 1 444	(e) 1 689	1 526	6.8
Seychelles	569	1 271	104	(e) 1 015	(e) 532	16 111	3.7
Sierra Leone	554	1 354	118	-	-	514	2.0
Somalia	(e) 340	(e) 1 240	106	405	1 478	(u) 108	3.3
South Africa	93 970	(e) 113 605	105	15 960	16 494	6 368	0.8
South Sudan	..	..	..	(e) 217	(e) 596	753	7.4
Sudan	3 485	7 850	104	1 511	1 172	980	-2.0
Togo	1 147	2 512	101	(e) 587	(e) 435	679	4.9
Tunisia	15 534	22 706	114	(e) 3 779	(e) 3 162	3 462	2.5
Uganda	3 087	6 729	95	(e) 1 960	(e) 2 545	687	6.1
United Republic of Tanzania	3 982	8 818	100	(e) 3 769	(e) 2 052	1 041	7.1
Western Sahara	..	..	..	..	..	..	..
Zambia	9 043	9 462	103	957	1 688	1 552	3.7
Zimbabwe	(e) 4 387	(e) 4 100	100	(e) 503	(e) 1 400	2 374	1.3
Developing economies: America	1 086 460	1 123 090	106	190 270	222 160	8 553	0.7
Anguilla	(e) 12	(e) 234	100	(e) 153	(e) 83	20 307	3.5
Antigua and Barbuda	87	501	95	(e) 1 082	(e) 471	16 818	5.3
Argentina	61 620	65 443	104	14 129	23 836	11 595	-2.5
Aruba	194	1 229	109	(e) 2 344	(e) 1 060	26 744	1.1
Bahamas	655	3 311	95	(e) 3 276	(e) 2 184	32 252	2.5
Barbados	448	1 578	96	1 348	521	16 936	-0.6
Belize	452	958	100	(e) 615	(e) 236	5 130	3.0
Bolivia (Plurinational State of)	8 965	9 996	101	1 466	3 256	3 598	4.4
Bonaire, Sint Eustatius and Saba	(e) 1	(e) 93	..	..	..	..	..
Brazil	239 889	188 564	107	34 023	67 975	8 928	1.1
British Virgin Islands	(e) 19	(e) 290	100	-	-	35 245	3.3
Cayman Islands	(e) 34	(e) 1 160	95	-	-	66 980	3.2
Chile	75 452	75 003	112	(e) 10 130	(e) 13 851	15 881	4.0
Colombia	41 774	51 233	127	(e) 9 308	(e) 13 324	6 656	2.7
Costa Rica	11 201	16 159	100	9 092	3 847	11 905	2.7
Cuba	(e) 2 820	(e) 10 040	105	(e) 10 737	(e) 2 182	9 232	1.1
Curaçao	609	1 786	-	(e) 1 409	(e) 1 172	..	-1.7
Dominica	18	302	100	(e) 155	(e) 138	6 720	-4.4
Dominican Republic	10 908	20 209	95	9 284	3 399	7 552	6.3
Ecuador	21 606	23 193	102	2 546	3 255	6 315	1.4
El Salvador	5 905	11 830	94	2 798	1 997	4 033	2.4
Falkland Islands (Malvinas)	(e) 276	(e) 138	103	..	..	..	..
Grenada	31	456	84	(e) 621	(e) 245	10 774	5.2

Current account balance	FDI		CPI growth	Population			Fleet size[b]	Economy
	Outflows	Inflows		Total	Share of urban	Old-age dependency ratio		
(Millions of US$)	(Millions of US$)	(Millions of US$)	(Percentage)	(Thousands)	(Percentage)	(Percentage)	(1000 of dwt)	
-265	76	196	4.3	2 448	50.0	6.1	33	Namibia
(e) -1 499	44	460	3.0	22 443	16.4	5.5	1	Niger
5 334	1 381	1 997	12.1	195 875	50.3	5.1	4 084	Nigeria
-747	18	398	-0.3	12 302	17.2	5.1	..	Rwanda
..	..	..	..	6	39.8	..	..	Saint Helena
-62	2	17	7.9	211	72.8	5.4	11	Sao Tome and Principe
(e) -2 789	73	629	0.5	15 854	47.2	5.7	14	Senegal
-269	6	124	3.7	97	56.7	11.0	205	Seychelles
-	..	599	16.9	7 650	42.1	5.3	2 151	Sierra Leone
..	..	409	..	15 008	45.0	5.7	1	Somalia
-13 381	4 552	5 334	4.5	57 793	66.4	8.1	441	South Africa
455	..	191	83.5	10 976	19.6	6.2	..	South Sudan
-4 679	..	1 136	63.3	41 802	34.6	6.4	5	Sudan
-	259	102	0.9	7 809	41.7	6.1	1 598	Togo
-4 429	34	1 036	7.3	11 565	68.9	12.3	307	Tunisia
-2 565	0	1 337	2.6	42 729	23.8	3.8	..	Uganda
(e) -2 141	..	1 105	3.5	56 313	33.8	4.9	819	United Republic of Tanzania
..	..	..	..	567	86.7	4.3	..	Western Sahara
-342	32	569	7.5	17 352	43.5	4.0	..	Zambia
(e) -519	27	745	10.6	14 439	32.2	5.4	..	Zimbabwe
-97 736	**6 515**	**146 720**	**8.3**	**638 014**	**80.5**	**12.5**	**449 483**	**Developing economies: America**
(p) -136	-1	56	2.8	15	100.0		4	Anguilla
(p) 113	9	116	1.3	96	24.6	12.7	7 501	Antigua and Barbuda
-27 479	1 911	12 162	34.3	44 361	91.9	17.3	607	Argentina
48	27	136	3.6	106	43.4	19.7	..	Aruba
(e) -1 988	119	943	2.3	386	83.0	10.3	77 844	Bahamas
-124	34	195	3.6	287	31.1	23.6	1 671	Barbados
-155	1	120	0.3	383	45.7	7.3	3 304	Belize
-1 990	-89	255	2.3	11 353	69.4	11.6	120	Bolivia (Plurinational State of)
..	..	..	..	26	74.9	..	..	Bonaire, Sint Eustatius and Saba
-14 970	-13 036	61 223	3.7	209 469	86.6	12.8	5 335	Brazil
..	56 019	44 244	2.1	30	47.7	..	5	British Virgin Islands
..	40 378	57 384	3.3	64	100.0	..	6 743	Cayman Islands
-9 157	3 027	7 160	2.4	18 729	87.6	16.8	1 166	Chile
-12 909	5 122	11 010	3.2	49 661	80.8	12.4	97	Colombia
-1 877	58	2 134	2.2	4 999	79.3	13.8	2	Costa Rica
-	..	..	6.9	11 338	77.0	22.1	35	Cuba
-899	45	124	2.6	163	89.1	25.9	1 509	Curaçao
(p) -225	0	-37	1.4	72	70.5	..	1 190	Dominica
-1 160	..	2 535	3.6	10 627	81.1	10.9	59	Dominican Republic
-1 487	..	1 401	-0.2	17 084	63.8	11.0	282	Ecuador
-1 242	0	840	1.1	6 421	72.0	12.8	..	El Salvador
..	..	..	..	3	77.7	..	6	Falkland Islands (Malvinas)
(p) -116	15	127	1.1	111	36.3	14.4	1	Grenada

Economy	Merchandise trade			Trade in services		GDP	
	Exports	Imports	Terms of trade	Exports	Imports	Per capita (nominal)	Growth (real)[a]
	(Millions of US$)	(Millions of US$)	(2015=100)	(Millions of US$)	(Millions of US$)	(US$)	(Percentage)
Guatemala	10 769	19 699	127	2 805	3 480	4 579	3.1
Guyana	1 374	1 825	106	-	-	4 710	3.4
Haiti	1 078	4 822	98	(e) 541	(e) 1 089	834	1.4
Honduras	8 669	12 200	129	2 879	2 139	2 484	3.7
Jamaica	1 879	6 126	107	(e) 3 828	(e) 2 524	5 288	1.5
Mexico	450 685	476 546	100	(e) 28 562	(e) 37 244	9 694	2.0
Montserrat	5	34	94	(e) 19	(e) 21	12 181	2.0
Nicaragua	5 014	6 629	112	1 343	929	2 048	-4.1
Panama	11 480	23 006	97	13 789	4 484	15 470	3.7
Paraguay	9 045	13 334	97	1 174	1 281	4 508	3.6
Peru	49 068	43 262	112	(e) 7 365	(e) 9 902	6 951	4.0
Saint Barthélemy	..	..	..	..	..	..	..
Saint Kitts and Nevis	54	335	94	(e) 597	(e) 262	18 073	2.1
Saint Lucia	133	684	95	(e) 983	(e) 372	9 927	2.5
Saint Martin (French part)	..	..	..	..	..	..	..
Saint Vincent and the Grenadines	45	354	97	(e) 271	(e) 139	7 541	3.2
Sint Maarten (Dutch part)	148	902	..	(e) 474	(e) 329	..	-8.4
Suriname	2 129	1 582	105	151	610	7 375	1.9
Trinidad and Tobago	(e) 9 990	(e) 7 090	99	(e) 1 170	(e) 2 814	16 345	1.9
Turks and Caicos Islands	(e) 4	(e) 362	105	(e) 655	(e) 60	28 589	2.6
Uruguay	7 503	8 893	97	4 922	3 739	17 352	1.6
Venezuela (Bolivarian Rep. of)	(e) 34 410	(e) 11 700	99	-	-	(e) 7 412	-15.0
Developing economies: Asia	7 072 252	6 607 999	98	1 425 120	1 713 230	5 990	5.3
Afghanistan	875	7 407	107	(e) 681	(e) 1 257	576	2.5
Bahrain	18 258	(e) 12 895	112	(e) 11 915	(e) 7 939	24 533	2.7
Bangladesh	39 252	60 495	92	(e) 5 501	(e) 10 829	1 671	7.9
Bhutan	606	1 048	106	185	237	3 609	6.9
Brunei Darussalam	6 574	4 164	115	(e) 581	(e) 1 574	32 804	-0.3
Cambodia	(e) 13 950	18 780	93	5 451	3 016	1 501	7.2
China	2 486 695	2 135 748	91	266 841	525 040	9 530	6.6
China, Hong Kong SAR	568 454	626 616	100	(e) 114 024	(e) 81 511	49 233	3.0
China, Macao SAR	1 510	11 162	100	(e) 43 585	(e) 5 083	86 914	5.8
China, Taiwan Province of	335 909	286 333	93	(e) 50 290	(e) 56 792	24 760	2.6
India	324 778	514 464	94	(e) 205 108	(e) 176 583	2 030	7.4
Indonesia	180 215	188 707	102	27 932	35 034	3 892	5.2
Iran (Islamic Republic of)	(e) 105 000	49 353	120	-	-	6 087	-0.3
Iraq	95 256	53 191	137	5 571	18 000	5 636	2.4
Jordan	7 773	20 216	106	(e) 7 281	(e) 4 793	4 242	1.9
Korea, Dem. People's Rep. of	(e) 300	(e) 2 590	113	-	-	-	-1.0
Korea, Republic of	604 860	535 202	95	(e) 96 601	(e) 124 262	31 657	2.7
Kuwait	71 938	35 864	120	(e) 8 175	(e) 35 081	33 905	1.2
Lao People's Dem. Rep.	5 295	6 164	104	(e) 921	(e) 1 154	2 574	6.7
Lebanon	3 830	20 396	102	(e) 15 355	(e) 14 371	8 277	0.9
Malaysia	247 455	217 602	97	(e) 39 641	(e) 44 550	11 237	4.7

Current account balance	FDI		CPI growth	Population			Fleet size[b]	Economy
	Outflows	Inflows		Total	Share of urban	Old-age dependency ratio		
(Millions of US$)	(Millions of US$)	(Millions of US$)	(Percentage)	(Thousands)	(Percentage)	(Percentage)	(1000 of dwt)	
638	235	1 056	3.8	17 248	51.1	7.9	1	Guatemala
-258	0	495	1.3	779	26.6	9.9	41	Guyana
-343	..	105	13.5	11 123	55.3	8.0	1	Haiti
-1 005	80	1 226	4.3	9 588	57.1	7.4	424	Honduras
-464	13	775	3.7	2 935	55.7	13.0	134	Jamaica
-21 643	6 858	31 604	4.9	126 191	80.2	10.9	2 288	Mexico
(p) -1	..	2	-0.6	5	9.1	..	..	Montserrat
83	75	359	4.9	6 466	58.5	8.1	6	Nicaragua
-5 067	158	5 549	0.8	4 177	67.7	12.5	333 337	Panama
220	..	454	4.0	6 956	61.6	10.0	83	Paraguay
-3 594	19	6 175	1.3	31 989	77.9	12.2	526	Peru
..	..	..	..	10	(e) 71.3	..	..	Saint Barthélemy
(p) -72	0	85	-0.6	52	30.8	..	804	Saint Kitts and Nevis
(p) 103	13	135	1.9	182	18.7	13.7		Saint Lucia
..	..	..	..	37	(e) 71.3	..	..	Saint Martin (French part)
(p) -99	-5	100	2.4	110	52.2	14.1	2 632	Saint Vincent and the Grenadines
63	5	145	..	42	100.0	..	..	Sint Maarten (Dutch part)
-189	..	190	6.9	576	66.1	10.5	7	Suriname
1 608	155	-436	1.1	1 390	53.2	15.6	18	Trinidad and Tobago
173	..	..	3.2	30	93.1		0	Turks and Caicos Islands
-348	273	-020	7.6	3 440	95.3	22.9	41	Uruguay
(e) 5 906	1 655	956	929 789.4	28 887	88.2	11.2	1 661	Venezuela (Bolivarian Rep. of)
337 397	401 407	511 707	4.0	4 334 938	48.6	11.4	548 647	Developing economies: Asia
-	6	139	0.6	37 172	25.5	4.8	..	Afghanistan
(e) -2 220	111	1 515	2.1	1 569	89.3	3.1	289	Bahrain
-7 593	23	3 613	5.5	161 377	36.6	7.7	2 449	Bangladesh
-498	..	6	2.7	754	40.9	8.8	..	Bhutan
1 068	..	504	0.2	429	77.6	6.8	458	Brunei Darussalam
-2 773	124	3 103	2.4	16 250	23.4	7.1	453	Cambodia
49 092	129 830	139 043	2.1	1 427 648	59.2	15.3	91 956	China
15 556	85 162	115 662	2.4	7 372	100.0	23.7	198 747	China, Hong Kong SAR
(e) 19 108	-496	1 113	3.0	632	100.0	13.8	2	China, Macao SAR
71 989	18 024	6 998	1.5	23 726	78.2	19.8	5 751	China, Taiwan Province of
-65 599	11 037	42 286	4.9	1 352 642	34.0	9.3	17 354	India
-31 051	8 139	21 980	3.2	267 671	55.3	8.7	23 880	Indonesia
19 489	75	3 480	31.2	81 800	74.9	8.9	4 257	Iran (Islamic Republic of)
35 270	188	-4 885	0.4	38 434	70.5	5.7	105	Iraq
-2 850	-8	950	4.5	9 965	91.0	6.2	102	Jordan
..	..	52	..	25 550	61.9	13.2	1 048	Korea, Dem. People's Rep. of
76 409	38 917	14 479	1.5	51 172	81.5	19.9	13 029	Korea, Republic of
24 049	3 751	346	0.7	4 137	100.0	3.4	4 159	Kuwait
-1 430	0	1 320	2.0	7 061	35.0	6.4	2	Lao People's Dem. Rep.
(e) -15 238	1 058	2 880	6.1	6 859	88.6	10.5	205	Lebanon
7 590	5 280	8 091	0.9	31 528	76.0	9.6	10 162	Malaysia

Economy	Merchandise trade			Trade in services		GDP	
	Exports	Imports	Terms of trade	Exports	Imports	Per capita (nominal)	Growth (real)[a]
	(Millions of US$)	(Millions of US$)	(2015=100)	(Millions of US$)	(Millions of US$)	(US$)	(Percentage)
Maldives	339	2 960	107	(e) 3 290	(e) 1 372	10 093	4.9
Mongolia	7 012	5 875	128	1 112	3 090	3 988	6.7
Myanmar	16 640	19 347	98	(e) 5 370	(e) 3 983	1 304	6.9
Nepal	786	12 714	90	(e) 2 101	(e) 2 323	971	6.8
Oman	(e) 46 637	(e) 25 412	92	-	-	17 115	2.6
Pakistan	23 485	60 472	91	5 255	10 123	1 326	5.2
Philippines	67 488	119 330	97	37 469	26 976	3 102	6.2
Qatar	84 288	31 696	110	18 273	32 504	68 932	1.4
Saudi Arabia	294 373	137 065	126	18 064	86 457	23 053	2.2
Singapore	412 953	370 881	95	184 015	186 956	60 322	3.2
Sri Lanka	11 890	22 233	106	(e) 8 412	(e) 6 831	4 168	3.2
State of Palestine	(e) 2 521	(e) 7 965	96	(e) 613	(e) 1 626	3 002	0.9
Syrian Arab Republic	(e) 2 000	(e) 6 400	98	-	-	1 152	10.1
Thailand	252 957	248 201	98	(e) 84 091	(e) 55 276	7 272	4.1
Timor-Leste	47	565	..	(e) 239	(e) 452	2 831	0.5
Turkey	167 921	223 047	96	48 750	23 371	9 312	2.6
United Arab Emirates	316 896	261 538	110	71 831	72 294	44 094	1.7
Viet Nam	242 683	235 517	98	(e) 15 106	(e) 18 399	2 559	6.9
Yemen	(e) 2 552	(e) 8 387	118	-	-	1 446	0.2
Developing economies: Oceania	14 453	14 648	106	-	-	4 290	1.4
American Samoa	(e) 430	(e) 610	93	-	-	..	..
Cook Islands	16	134	..	-	-	17 557	2.0
Fiji	1 041	2 720	100	1 591	722	5 795	3.0
French Polynesia	148	2 236	94	-	-	21 426	2.0
Guam	34	(e) 1 070	105	-	-	..	..
Kiribati	(e) 13	(e) 120	109	-	-	1 730	2.3
Marshall Islands	(e) 42	(e) 75	103	-	-	3 488	1.5
Micronesia (Federated States of)	(e) 75	(e) 110	104	-	-	3 062	1.5
Nauru	(e) 16	(e) 118	97	-	-	11 077	4.0
New Caledonia	1 935	2 807	112	-	-	38 404	2.4
Niue	(e) 2	(e) 19	93	-	-	..	..
Northern Mariana Islands	(e) 5	(e) 175	109	-	-	..	..
Palau	(e) 8	(e) 155	99	-	-	16 583	0.0
Papua New Guinea	10 041	2 600	106	(e) 404	(e) 1 705	2 681	0.0
Samoa	46	363	101	-	-	4 508	1.7
Solomon Islands	524	(e) 615	97	(e) 158	(e) 201	1 982	3.3
Tokelau	(e) 0	(e) 0	87	..	..	..	..
Tonga	(e) 15	(e) 270	99	89	106	4 250	2.0
Tuvalu	(e) 0	(e) 36	-	(e) 3	(e) 14	3 969	3.0
Vanuatu	63	350	92	-	-	3 037	2.2
Wallis and Futuna Islands	(e) 0	(e) 65	102	..	..	..	..
Transition economies	674 171	491 583	116	137 210	158 100	7 332	2.8
Albania	2 870	5 925	102	3 613	2 309	5 306	4.2
Armenia	2 412	4 963	110	2 063	2 211	4 274	5.2

| Current account balance | FDI | | CPI growth | Population | | | Fleet size[b] | Economy |
| | Outflows | Inflows | | Total | Share of urban | Old-age dependency ratio | | |
(Millions of US$)	(Millions of US$)	(Millions of US$)	(Percentage)	(Thousands)	(Percentage)	(Percentage)	(1000 of dwt)	
-1 338	..	552	-0.1	516	39.8	4.8	66	Maldives
-1 903	37	2 174	6.8	3 170	68.4	6.2	733	Mongolia
-2 137	..	3 554	6.9	53 708	30.6	8.5	168	Myanmar
-	..	161	4.2	28 096	19.7	9.0	..	Nepal
-4 347	567	4 191	0.9	4 829	84.5	3.2	15	Oman
-19 191	8	2 352	5.1	212 228	36.7	7.1	709	Pakistan
-7 879	602	6 456	5.2	106 651	46.9	8.0	5 428	Philippines
16 652	3 523	-2 186	0.2	2 782	99.1	1.6	1 159	Qatar
70 606	21 219	3 209	2.5	33 703	83.8	4.6	13 128	Saudi Arabia
65 072	37 143	77 646	0.4	5 758	100.0	15.0	129 581	Singapore
2 814	68	1 611	2.1	21 229	18.5	16.0	417	Sri Lanka
-1 659	75	226	-0.2	4 863	76.2	5.4	..	State of Palestine
-1 980	..	..	3.4	16 945	54.2	7.0	75	Syrian Arab Republic
35 159	17 714	10 493	1.1	69 428	49.0	10.0	5 732	Thailand
(p) -90	..	40	2.3	1 268	30.6	7.5	0	Timor-Leste
-27 252	3 608	12 944	16.3	82 340	75.1	12.7	7 489	Turkey
(e) 28 028	15 079	10 385	3.1	9 631	86.5	1.3	628	United Arab Emirates
5 899	598	15 500	3.5	95 546	35.9	10.5	8 469	Viet Nam
-1	4	-282	41.8	28 499	36.6	5.0	441	Yemen
4 507	220	1 713	2.8	11 930	22.8	6.6	254 647	Developing economies: Oceania
..	..	..	..	55	87.2	..	..	American Samoa
..	0	5	0.1	18	75.0	..	2 626	Cook Islands
-486	-4	344	4.1	883	56.2	8.4	66	Fiji
..	22	59	-0.7	278	61.8	12.0	16	French Polynesia
..	..	..	..	166	94.8	15.0	0	Guam
-	0	1	1.9	116	54.1	6.5	238	Kiribati
8	..	-1	0.8	58	77.0	..	245 763	Marshall Islands
80	..	..	2.0	113	22.7	6.2	69	Micronesia (Federated States of)
..	..	..	3.8	11	100.0	..	12	Nauru
..	83	874	1.3	280	70.7	13.5	10	New Caledonia
..	..	..	..	2	44.8	..	279	Niue
..	..	..	..	57	91.6	..	..	Northern Mariana Islands
..	1	22	2.8	18	79.9	..	1 328	Palau
(e) 5 007	-343	335	4.7	8 606	13.2	5.7	172	Papua New Guinea
-	0	17	4.2	196	18.2	8.4	20	Samoa
-51	9	12	1.0	653	23.7	6.4	4	Solomon Islands
..	..	..	..	1	0.0	..	..	Tokelau
-29	1	8	3.9	103	23.1	10.2	36	Tonga
2		0	4.2	12	62.4	..	1 899	Tuvalu
-64	1	38	2.8	293	25.3	6.3	2 109	Vanuatu
..	..	..	..	12	0.0	..	..	Wallis and Futuna Islands
102 925	38 174	34 218	4.1	310 161	65.3	18.6	11 304	Transition economies
-1 008	83	1 294	2.0	2 883	60.3	20.0	48	Albania
-1 165	-12	254	2.5	2 952	63.1	16.5	..	Armenia

Economy	Merchandise trade			Trade in services		GDP	
	Exports	Imports	Terms of trade	Exports	Imports	Per capita (nominal)	Growth (real)[a]
	(Millions of US$)	(Millions of US$)	(2015=100)	(Millions of US$)	(Millions of US$)	(US$)	(Percentage)
Azerbaijan	(e) 19 720	(e) 11 490	126	4 691	6 753	4 567	1.4
Belarus	33 726	38 409	102	8 721	5 376	6 277	3.0
Bosnia and Herzegovina	7 182	11 628	100	2 097	616	5 975	3.0
Georgia	3 356	9 137	106	4 490	2 246	4 099	4.7
Kazakhstan	60 956	32 534	124	7 275	11 871	9 110	4.1
Kyrgyzstan	1 779	5 089	107	(e) 834	(e) 970	1 261	3.5
Montenegro	472	3 010	..	1 832	738	8 630	4.9
North Macedonia	6 911	9 050	97	1 845	1 418	6 086	2.7
Republic of Moldova	2 706	5 760	99	1 468	1 095	2 366	4.0
Russian Federation	443 129	248 704	122	(e) 64 859	(e) 94 658	11 179	2.3
Serbia	19 227	25 882	97	8 710	6 520	6 363	4.3
Tajikistan	(e) 1 160	(e) 3 150	115	242	458	827	7.1
Turkmenistan	(e) 10 000	(e) 2 500	112	-	-	7 535	6.2
Ukraine	47 348	57 046	101	15 772	14 367	2 816	3.3
Uzbekistan	11 218	17 306	103	(e) 4 283	(e) 1 241	1 272	5.1
Developed economies	10 122 086	10 980 183	100	3 969 720	3 327 310	46 378	2.2
Developed economies: America	2 117 242	3 084 963	100	922 850	673 100	60 740	2.7
Bermuda	18	1 100	114	(e) 1 546	(e) 1 029	102 987	1.4
Canada	450 585	470 558	102	(e) 92 881	(e) 112 855	46 080	1.8
Greenland	641	829	104	-	-	52 350	1.5
Saint Pierre and Miquelon	7	97	101	-	-	..	..
United States of America	1 665 992	2 612 379	100	(e) 828 428	(e) 559 213	62 380	2.8
Developed economies: Asia	800 095	828 588	97	241 940	230 820	39 485	0.9
Israel	61 952	(e) 80 100	95	(e) 49 929	(e) 30 773	44 134	3.3
Japan	738 143	748 488	97	(e) 192 006	(e) 200 047	39 178	0.8
Developed economies: Europe	6 907 978	6 787 454	99	2 718 860	2 337 810	37 645	2.0
Andorra	(e) 122	(e) 1 381	..	..	..	41 482	0.5
Austria	184 815	193 722	97	(e) 74 144	(e) 61 648	51 437	2.7
Belgium	466 724	450 075	98	(e) 123 405	(e) 128 904	46 375	1.4
Bulgaria	33 141	37 881	98	(e) 9 922	(e) 6 026	9 195	3.1
Croatia	17 402	28 203	96	(e) 16 551	(e) 5 324	14 586	2.6
Cyprus	4 996	10 774	101	(e) 11 904	(e) 7 074	28 017	3.9
Czechia	202 261	184 652	100	(e) 29 927	(e) 24 651	22 677	2.9
Denmark	109 120	102 566	99	(e) 69 578	(e) 68 602	61 110	1.4
Estonia	17 025	19 124	101	(e) 7 685	(e) 5 513	22 306	3.9
Faroe Islands	1 271	1 226	105	-	-	..	..
Finland	75 841	78 636	97	(e) 32 704	(e) 35 474	49 735	2.3
France	581 872	672 549	97	(e) 291 494	(e) 256 773	41 376	1.6
Germany	1 560 648	1 285 722	99	(e) 331 156	(e) 351 455	48 057	1.4
Gibraltar	(e) 150	(e) 850	86	-	-	..	..
Greece	39 478	63 810	99	(e) 43 188	(e) 20 986	20 764	1.9
Holy See	..	..	..	..	..	..	..
Hungary	125 795	121 682	102	(e) 29 204	(e) 20 190	16 033	4.9
Iceland	5 556	7 679	110	(e) 6 482	(e) 4 208	76 809	4.6

Current account balance	FDI		CPI growth	Population			Fleet size[b]	Economy
	Outflows	Inflows		Total	Share of urban	Old-age dependency ratio		
(Millions of US$)	(Millions of US$)	(Millions of US$)	(Percentage)	(Thousands)	(Percentage)	(Percentage)	(1000 of dwt)	
6 051	1 761	1 403	1.9	9 950	55.7	8.8	765	Azerbaijan
-266	36	1 469	4.9	9 453	78.6	21.7	1	Belarus
-829	18	468	1.4	3 324	48.2	24.0	..	Bosnia and Herzegovina
-1 246	340	1 232	2.6	4 003	58.6	22.8	143	Georgia
-52	-1 103	3 817	6.0	18 320	57.4	11.5	102	Kazakhstan
-700	1	47	1.5	6 304	36.4	7.1	..	Kyrgyzstan
-943	103	490	2.6	628	66.8	22.4	140	Montenegro
-46	3	737	1.5	2 083	58.0	19.6	..	North Macedonia
-1 187	31	228	3.0	4 052	42.6	15.8	502	Republic of Moldova
113 455	36 445	13 332	2.9	145 734	74.4	21.8	9 132	Russian Federation
-2 630	416	4 378	2.0	8 803	56.1	27.8	..	Serbia
-379	57	317	3.8	9 101	27.1	5.0	..	Tajikistan
1 388	..	1 985	13.6	5 851	51.6	6.8	121	Turkmenistan
-4 287	-5	2 355	11.0	44 246	69.4	24.3	350	Ukraine
-	..	412	17.9	32 476	50.5	6.6	..	Uzbekistan
99 728	558 445	556 892	1.9	1 061 270	80.3	29.9	448 936	Developed economies
-535 416	-13 126	291 512	2.4	367 440	82.3	24.3	24 220	Developed economies: America
-	-31	73	1.7	63	100.0	..	9 088	Bermuda
-45 323	50 455	39 625	2.3	37 075	81.4	25.8	3 318	Canada
		..	0.0	57	86.8	..	1	Greenland
..	..	..	..	6	90.2	..	..	Saint Pierre and Miquelon
-490 991	-63 550	251 814	2.4	330 241	82.4	24.2	11 812	United States of America
184 630	149 169	31 661	1.0	135 584	91.7	44.5	39 345	Developed economies: Asia
9 912	6 008	21 803	0.8	8 382	92.4	19.9	312	Israel
174 719	143 161	9 858	1.0	127 202	91.6	46.2	39 034	Japan
487 129	418 363	171 877	1.8	528 604	75.7	30.7	382 766	Developed economies: Europe
..	..	..	0.7	77	88.1	..	..	Andorra
10 801	-747	7 618	2.0	8 891	58.3	28.5	..	Austria
-6 819	6 910	4 873	2.1	11 482	98.0	29.3	10 471	Belgium
2 959	387	2 059	2.8	7 052	75.0	32.7	147	Bulgaria
1 459	354	1 159	1.5	4 156	56.9	31.4	2 057	Croatia
-1 685	-2 237	3 285	1.4	870	66.8	19.7	34 588	Cyprus
860	5 277	9 479	2.1	10 666	73.8	29.9	..	Czechia
19 977	-3 690	1 789	0.8	5 752	87.9	31.1	22 497	Denmark
571	-22	1 309	3.4	1 323	68.9	30.7	80	Estonia
..	..	..	..	48	42.1	..	409	Faroe Islands
-4 393	10 961	1 225	1.1	5 523	85.4	35.0	1 106	Finland
-17 864	102 421	37 294	1.9	67 230	80.7	31.9	7 265	France
291 199	77 076	25 706	1.7	83 124	77.3	33.1	8 470	Germany
..	..	..	..	34	100.0	..	2 226	Gibraltar
-6 290	848	4 257	0.6	10 522	79.1	33.7	69 101	Greece
..	..	..	..	1	100.0	..	..	Holy See
627	1 991	6 389	2.9	9 708	71.4	28.8	0	Hungary
731	138	-336	2.7	337	93.8	22.6	18	Iceland

Economy	Merchandise trade			Trade in services		GDP	
	Exports	Imports	Terms of trade	Exports	Imports	Per capita (nominal)	Growth (real)[a]
	(Millions of US$)	(Millions of US$)	(2015=100)	(Millions of US$)	(Millions of US$)	(US$)	(Percentage)
Ireland	164 871	107 614	94	(e) 205 732	(e) 218 083	77 307	6.7
Italy	546 643	500 795	98	(e) 121 589	(e) 124 980	34 170	0.9
Latvia	16 128	19 671	102	(e) 6 219	(e) 3 401	18 076	4.8
Lithuania	33 337	36 502	99	(e) 11 568	(e) 6 860	19 000	3.4
Luxembourg	16 292	24 024	94	(e) 113 139	(e) 86 297	113 314	2.6
Malta	3 012	6 323	95	(e) 15 061	(e) 10 660	32 601	6.6
Netherlands	723 752	644 673	99	(e) 242 489	(e) 228 851	53 550	2.7
Norway	121 791	86 600	108	42 868	51 837	81 477	1.4
Poland	260 607	266 504	98	(e) 69 246	(e) 43 302	15 452	5.1
Portugal	68 490	88 575	99	(e) 37 662	(e) 18 271	20 667	2.1
Romania	79 671	97 778	98	(e) 26 611	(e) 16 813	12 322	4.1
San Marino	..	..	..	..	..	53 686	1.1
Slovakia	94 267	93 891	103	(e) 11 533	(e) 10 624	19 524	4.1
Slovenia	44 200	42 267	98	(e) 9 395	(e) 5 706	26 083	4.5
Spain	345 166	388 044	98	(e) 149 167	(e) 85 391	30 518	2.6
Sweden	165 937	170 167	97	(e) 73 135	(e) 68 870	55 302	2.4
Switzerland, Liechtenstein	310 749	279 528	103	124 275	103 402	82 904	2.5
United Kingdom	486 850	673 965	103	(e) 376 157	(e) 235 339	41 794	1.4
Developed economies: Oceania	296 770	279 178	117	86 070	85 590	55 477	2.8
Australia	257 098	235 386	119	(e) 69 171	(e) 71 851	57 830	2.8
New Zealand	39 673	43 793	109	(e) 16 899	(e) 13 736	43 127	2.8
Selected groups							
Developing economies excluding China	6 170 410	6 186 210	103	1 471 290	1 593 170	4 186	3.0
Developing economies excluding LDCs	8 465 698	8 050 960	99	1 692 440	2 041 410	6 241	4.2
LDCs	191 406	270 998	107	45 690	76 800	1 061	4.7
LLDCs	190 870	214 709	112	47 580	68 310	1 537	4.6
SIDS (UNCTAD)	18 645	37 379	102	24 510	16 260	7 855	2.4
HIPCs (IMF)	130 116	177 590	107	38 240	64 160	944	5.1
BRICS	3 588 462	3 201 085	96	586 790	880 750	6 331	5.4
G20	14 928 292	15 304 094	99	4 542 880	4 310 990	15 232	3.0

[a] At constant 2010 United States dollars.
[b] As of 1 January 2019.

| Current account balance | FDI | | CPI growth | Population | | | Fleet size[b] | Economy |
| | Outflows | Inflows | | Total | Share of urban | Old-age dependency ratio | | |
(Millions of US$)	(Millions of US$)	(Millions of US$)	(Percentage)	(Thousands)	(Percentage)	(Percentage)	(1000 of dwt)	
34 243	13 272	-66 346	0.5	4 819	63.2	21.4	342	Ireland
50 556	20 576	24 276	1.1	60 627	70.4	35.6	13 409	Italy
-296	150	879	2.5	1 928	68.1	31.3	75	Latvia
817	838	905	2.7	2 801	67.7	30.1	178	Lithuania
3 389	1 373	-5 615	1.5	604	91.0	20.3	1 623	Luxembourg
1 433	-7 326	4 061	1.2	439	94.6	31.1	110 682	Malta
99 063	58 983	69 659	1.7	17 060	91.5	29.7	7 192	Netherlands
35 187	908	-18 215	2.8	5 338	82.2	26.1	21 865	Norway
-3 280	864	11 476	1.8	37 922	60.1	26.0	97	Poland
-1 508	271	4 895	1.0	10 256	65.2	34.0	19 662	Portugal
-10 757	13	5 888	4.6	19 506	54.0	27.7	60	Romania
..	..	..	1.6	34	97.2	..	..	San Marino
-2 614	234	475	2.5	5 453	53.7	22.7	..	Slovakia
3 073	82	1 419	1.7	2 078	54.5	30.0	1	Slovenia
12 797	31 620	43 601	1.7	46 693	80.3	29.4	1 891	Spain
9 458	20 028	11 148	2.0	9 972	87.4	32.2	1 067	Sweden
72 186	26 928	-87 212	0.9	8 564	73.5	28.0	1 226	Switzerland, Liechtenstein
-108 752	49 880	64 487	2.3	67 396	83.2	28.8	44 964	United Kingdom
-36 616	4 039	61 842	1.9	29 641	86.1	24.1	2 604	Developed economies: Oceania
-29 062	3 635	60 438	1.9	24 898	86.0	24.0	2 429	Australia
-7 553	404	1 404	1.6	4 743	86.5	24.2	176	New Zealand
								Selected groups
118 313	287 724	566 999	6.5	4 832 013	48.0	9.1	1 420 481	Developing economies excluding China
212 410	416 527	682 209	4.7	5 249 970	53.8	11.3	1 255 138	Developing economies excluding LDCs
-45 012	1 027	23 833	13.7	1 000 691	33.6	6.2	257 299	LDCs
-22 179	1 058	22 641	7.9	508 906	30.8	6.5	2 764	LLDCs
-4 738	247	1 999	2.4	12 811	45.8	11.2	344 852	SIDS (UNCTAD)
-35 057	1 333	27 144	6.3	719 972	35.9	5.5	250 279	HIPCs (IMF)
68 596	168 828	261 219	2.8	3 193 286	51.1	12.8	124 218	BRICS
96 555	773 570	996 971	2.7	4 831 991	59.7	16.1	598 255	G20

6.2 Classifications

Classification of economies

There is no established convention for the designation of "developing", "transition" and "developed" countries or areas in the United Nations system. The designation of economies used in this handbook is the classification used by UNCTAD. The differentiation between developing and developed economies follows, in general, the definition of the M49 classification (United Nations, 2019e). However, there are exceptions. Notably, the group 'transition economies' that was established to take account of the particular circumstances of that group of economies; shaped by socialism and now in transition to a market economy. The geographic locations of developing, transition and developed economies are depicted by the map titled "The world by development status" presented in the opening pages of this handbook.

Throughout the handbook, the group of developing economies is further broken down into the following three regions: "Africa", "America", "Asia and Oceania", where the group of African developing economies coincides with Africa, and the group of American developing economies coincides with Latin America and the Caribbean, as defined in M49. Apart from these five groups of economies, whenever possible, data are also presented for the following groups:

- Developing economies excluding China,

- Developing economies excluding LDCs,

- LDCs, according to the United Nations Office of the High Representative for the Least Developed Countries, Landlocked Developing Countries and the Small Island Developing States (UN-OHRLLS) (United Nations, 2019f),

- LLDCs, according to UN-OHRLLS (ibid.),

- SIDS according to UNCTAD (2019d),

- HIPCs, according to the International Monetary Fund (2019),

- Brazil, Russia, India, China and South Africa (BRICS),

- Group of Twenty (G20) (Japan, 2019).

The UNCTADstat classification page (UNCTAD, 2019a) provides the lists of the economies included in the different groups.

Classification of goods

For breakdowns of international merchandise trade by *product*, UNCTADstat applies the SITC, Revision 3, (United Nations, 1991) and various aggregates compiled on the basis of that classification. In this handbook, in chapter 1, reference is made to the following five product groups:

- All food items (SITC codes: 0, 1, 22, 4),

- Agricultural raw materials (SITC code 2 without 22, 27 and 28),

- Ores, metals, precious stones and non-monetary gold (SITC codes: 27, 28, 68, 667, 971),

- Fuels (SITC code 3),

- Manufactured goods (SITC codes: 5, 6, 7, 8 without 667 and 68).

For the measurement of movements in *commodity* prices in section 4.1, the FMCPI is disaggregated by commodity groups constructed from HS 2007 (World Customs Organization, 2006). For the correspondence between these commodity groups and HS headings and for the individual price quotations represented therein, see UNCTAD (2018).

Classification of services

The breakdown by service category in section 2.2 is based on EBOPS 2010 (United Nations et al., 2012). The EBOPS 2010 main categories have been grouped as shown in table 6.2 below.

Table 6.2 | Grouping of service categories on the basis of EBOPS 2010

EBOPS 2010	Section 2.2
Transport	Transport
Travel	Travel
Insurance and pension services	Insurance, financial, intellectual property, and other business services
Financial services	
Charges for the use of intellectual property n.i.e.	
Other business services	
Telecommunications, computer and information services	Telecommunications, computer and information
Personal, cultural and recreational services	Other categories
Government goods and services n.i.e.	
Construction	
Services not allocated	
Manufacturing services on physical inputs owned by others	
Maintenance and repair services n.i.e.	

Classification of economic activities

In section 3.1, gross value added is broken down by the three broad groups of economic activities below, in accordance with the International Standard Industrial Classification of All Economic Activities (ISIC), Revision 3 (United Nations, 1989):

- Agriculture, comprising: agriculture, hunting, forestry and fishing (ISIC divisions 01–05),
- Industry, comprising: mining and quarrying, manufacturing, electricity, gas and water supply, construction (ISIC divisions 10–45),
- Services, comprising all other economic activities (ISIC divisions 50–99).

6.3 Calculation methods

The **annual average growth rate** is, unless otherwise specified, computed as the coefficient b in the exponential trend function $y = ae^{bt}$ where t stands for time and y is the object of measurement. This method takes all observations in the analysed period into account. Therefore, the growth rate reflects trends that are less influenced by exceptional values.

In chapter 4, annual population growth is expressed by the **annual exponential rate of growth**, defined as:

$$b = ln\left(\frac{y_t}{y_{t-1}}\right)$$

The **trade openness index** (map 1.4) is calculated as the ratio of the arithmetic mean of merchandise exports (x) and imports (m) to GDP (y):

$$TOI_{i,t} = \frac{\frac{1}{2}(x_{i,t} + m_{i,t})}{y_{i,t}}$$

where i designates the economy and t the year.

The **terms of trade index** (figure 1.4.1, tables 1.4.1, 1.4.2) with base year 2015 is calculated as follows:

$$ToT_{i,t} = 100 \, \frac{\frac{UVI_{exports,i,t}}{UVI_{imports,i,t}}}{\frac{UVI_{exports,i,2015}}{UVI_{imports,i,2015}}}$$

where $UVI_{exports,i,t}$ is the unit value index of exports and $UVI_{imports,i,t}$ the unit value index of imports of economy i at time t.

The **market concentration index of exports** (figure 1.4.2) is calculated as a normalized Herfindahl-Hirschmann index:

$$MCI_{exports,i} = \frac{\sqrt{\sum_{j=1}^{n}\left(\frac{x_{i,j}}{X_i}\right)^2} - \sqrt{\frac{1}{n}}}{1 - \sqrt{\frac{1}{n}}}, \text{ with } X_i = \sum_{j=1}^{n} x_{i,j}$$

where $x_{i,j}$ is the value of exports of product i from economy j and n is the number of economies.

The **volume index of exports (imports)** (figure 1.4.3, tables 1.4.1 and 1.4.2) is calculated by dividing the export (import) value index by the corresponding unit value index and scaling up by 100:

$$QI_{i,t} = 100 \, \frac{VI_{i,t}}{UVI_{i,t}}$$

where $VI_{i,t}$ is the value index of exports (imports), given by

$$VI_{i,t} = 100 \, \frac{x_{i,t}}{x_{i,2015}}$$

$x_{i,t}$ is the value of exports (imports), $UVI_{i,t}$ is the unit value index of exports (imports), i designates the economy and t the time period.

The **purchasing power index of exports** (table 1.4.1) is calculated by dividing the export value index by the corresponding import unit value index and scaling up by 100:

$$PPI_{exports,i,t} = 100 \, \frac{VI_{exports,i,t}}{UVI_{imports,i,t}}$$

where $VI_{exports,i,t}$ is the value index of exports (as defined above), $UVI_{imports,i,t}$ is the unit value index of imports, i designates the economy and t the time period.

The **Lorenz curve** in figure 3.1.3 plots cumulative population shares ordered by GDP per capita, on the x-axis, against the cumulative shares of global GDP which they account for, on the y-axis. For the construction of the Lorenz curve, the n economies of the world are ordered with reference to their GDP per capita, so that

$$\frac{y_i}{p_i} \geq \frac{y_{i-1}}{p_{i-1}} \text{ for all } i \in \{2, 3, ..., n\}$$

where y_i is GDP and p_i the population of the economy at position i in this ranking, counted from below.

The cumulative population shares, measured on the x-axis, are calculated as

$$P_i = \sum_{j=1}^{i} \frac{p_j}{p} \quad \text{with } p = p_1 + p_2 + ... + p_n$$

The cumulative shares of global GDP, measured on the y-axis, are calculated as follows:

$$Y_i = \sum_{j=1}^{i} \frac{y_j}{y} \quad \text{with } y = y_1 + y_2 + ... + y_n$$

The **free market commodity price index** (section 3.4) is a fixed base-weight Laspeyres index with base-year 2015=100. It is calculated as

$$L_t = \frac{\sum_{i=1}^{n} p_{i,t} \, q_{i,2015}}{\sum_{i=1}^{n} p_{i,2015} \, q_{i,2015}}$$

where i is the identifier of the commodity group, $q_{i,2015}$ is the quantity for which products of commodity group i were exported by developing economies during the three years around the base year (from 2014 to 2016), and $p_{i,t}$ is the price of a representative product, within commodity group i, in year t. For more details, see UNCTAD (2018).

The **nowcasts** of world merchandise exports (section 1.1), world services exports (section 2.1) and world real GDP (section 3.1) represent real-time evaluations of these variables based on a large set of relevant and timely indicators. It is based on a dynamic factor model which captures common latent trends in these data through their cross correlations. In its state-space representation, the model can be written as:

$$G_t = Bh_t + u_t$$

$$h_t = Dh_{t-1} + v_t$$

where G_t is a combination of the reference and indicator series, h_t is the time-varying factor, B is a matrix of factor loadings, D defines the time structure of the factor, and the error terms u_t and v_t are independently distributed according to distributions N(0,W) and N(0,Q), respectively. The nowcast for the target variable at time t is obtained by extracting the corresponding element from vector G_t above, once B and the latent factor h_t have been estimated through maximum likelihood. This model is adapted to accommodate variables of different frequencies and unbalanced datasets. It should be noted that the nowcast figures cannot be considered as official data, as they are the result of an estimation. For more details on the methodology, see Cantú (2018).

6.4 References

Cantú F (2018). *Estimation of a Coincident Indicator for International Trade and Global Economic Activity.* UNCTAD Research Paper, No. 27, UNCTAD/SER.RP/2018/9.

International Monetary Fund (2009). *Balance of Payments and International Investment Position Manual. Sixth Edition (BPM6).* Washington, D.C.

International Monetary Fund (2019). Debt Relief under the Heavily Indebted Poor Countries (HIPC) Initiative. Available at https://www.imf.org/en/About/Factsheets/Sheets/2016/08/01/16/11/Debt-Relief-Under-the-Heavily-Indebted-Poor-Countries-Initiative.

Japan (2019). G20 Members. Available at https://g20.org/en/summit/about.

UNCTAD (2018). Free Market Commodity Price Index. Methodological Note. *Commodity Price Bulletin*, UNCTAD/STAT/CPB/MN/1. Available at https://unctad.org/en/PublicationsLibrary/statcpbmn1_en.pdf.

UNCTAD (2019a). UNCTADstat. See http://unctadstat.unctad.org.

UNCTAD (2019b). *World Investment Report 2019: Special Economic Zones.* United Nations publication. Sales No. E.19.II.D.12.

UNCTAD (2019c). *Review of Maritime Transport 2019.* United Nations publication. Sales no. E.19.II.D.20.

UNCTAD (2019d). UNCTAD's Unofficial List of SIDS. Available at https://unctad.org/en/pages/aldc/Small%20Island%20Developing%20States/UNCTAD%C2%B4s-unofficial-list-of-SIDS.aspx.

United Nations (1989). *International Standard Industrial Classification of All Economic Activities. Revision 3.* Department of International Economic and Social Affairs, Statistics Division, Statistical Papers, ST/ESA/STAT/SER.M/4/Rev.3. United Nations publication. Sales No. E.90.XVII.11.

United Nations (1991). *Standard International Trade Classification, Rev.3.* Department of International Economic and Social Affairs, Statistical Office, Statistical Papers, ST/ESA/STAT/SER.M/34/Rev.3. United Nations publication. Sales no. E.86.XVII.12.

United Nations (2011). *International Merchandise Trade Statistics: Concepts and Definitions 2010.* Department of Economic and Social Affairs, Statistics Division, Statistical Papers, ST/ESA/STAT/SER.M/52/Rev.3. United Nations publication. Sales No. E.10.XVII.13.

United Nations (2019a). UN Comtrade Database. See https://comtrade.un.org.

United Nations (2019b). *World Population Prospects 2019: Highlights.* Department of Economic and Social Affairs, Population Division. United Nations publication. Sales no. E.19.XIII.4.

United Nations (2019c). *World Population Prospects 2019: Data Booklet.* Department of Economic and Social Affairs, ST/ESA/SER.A/424.

United Nations (2019d). *World Urbanization Prospects 2018: Highlights.* Department of Economic and Social Affairs, Population Division. United Nations publication. Sales no. E19.XIII.6.

United Nations (2019e). Methodology: Standard Country or Area Codes for Statistical Use (M49). Available at https://unstats.un.org/unsd/methodology/m49.

United Nations (2019f). UN-OHRLLS. See http://unohrlls.org.

United Nations, European Commission, International Monetary Fund, Organisation for Economic Co-operation and Development, World Bank (2009). *System of National Accounts 2008.* ST/ESA/STAT/SER.F/2/Rev.5. Sales No. E.08.XVII.29.

United Nations, Statistical Office of the European Union, International Monetary Fund, Organisation for Economic Co-operation and Development, UNCTAD, World Tourism Organization, World Trade Organization (2012). *Manual on Statistics of International Trade in Services 2010.* ST/ESA/M.86/Rev. 1. United Nations publication. Sales No. E.10.XVII.14, Geneva.

World Customs Organization (2006). *Amendments to the Harmonized System Nomenclature. Effective from 1 January 2007.* D/2006/0448/10, Brussels.